GOD'S DIVINE AVALANCHE™

Preparing the Heart for Sudden Abundance

Frances Aurelia Newman

REFRANCA
PRESS
2026
USA

GOD'S DIVINE AVALANCHE™

Preparing the Heart for Sudden Abundance

First Edition
Published by Refranca Press
United States of America
ISBN: 978-0-692-98124-5
LCCN: 2026914553

Book cover design by Svitlana Stefaniuk.
All interior illustrations by Diletta De Santis.

Scripture quotations are taken from *The New Oxford Annotated Bible,* New Revised Standard Version, Fifth Edition, unless otherwise noted. This edition follows academic conventions, including the use of lowercase pronouns when referring to God. However, in the standalone devotional prayers set apart for reader use, divine pronouns and titles have been capitalized to reflect the pastoral character of those intentions.

For my husband, Nemo,
whose patience and love have steadied every season—
and for my three rivers,
John, James, and Julian,
whose lives have flowed through mine
and shaped this journey with grace.

ACKNOWLEDGMENTS

SPIRITUAL formation is never a solitary journey. I owe deep gratitude to the many people and communities whose prayers, wisdom, and companionship helped shape the heart of this book.

I am grateful to Fuller Theological Seminary, whose ecumenical community helped shape my spiritual, emotional, and theological formation by encouraging dialogue among believers from different Christian traditions—Catholic and Protestant together—wrestling honestly with faith, suffering, and calling.

I also wish to thank the many Protestant pastors, teachers, and friends who walked beside me during some of the most formative years of my faith. Although I was baptized Catholic in Our Lady of Esperanza, a church that still stands in the Upper Manhattan neighborhood of Washington Heights, my college years led me into the Protestant world, where faithful believers introduced me to a deep love of Scripture, contemporary worship, and a personal, living relationship with Jesus Christ. For four decades, those communities taught me to study the Bible diligently, to pray expectantly, and to follow Christ with sincerity. Their devotion shaped my early spiritual foundation in ways for which I remain profoundly grateful. The *sola scriptura* emphasis on the primacy of God's Word planted truths in me that would later blossom more fully as God continued guiding my journey.

My thanks also to Queen of Peace Catholic Church, to the humble priests and spiritual directors, my lovely OCIA classmates, my gracious sponsors, and all my new friends whose prayers and guidance helped me rediscover the Holy Family, the witness of the saints, the beauty of contemplative prayer, a renewed reverence for the sacraments, the gift of Eucharistic Adoration, and a deeper devotion to Christ.

In an avalanche bed, anchors are the trees and roots that break through the snow, stabilizing what would otherwise give way. In the same way, there have been anchors who held me steady through life's storms. Your presence, strength, and faith kept me from slipping when the ground beneath me felt uncertain. A thank you is not enough.

To my extended family, who model the many facets of Christianity like a prism, reflecting God's light in countless colors, each one revealing something beautiful and true—thank you!

To my fur babies, my rainbow bridge dogs and my Toby (you couldn't read a single page, but you never left my side while I wrote them), a big hug and kiss from mama.

And to you, the reader. Thank you for your openness and courage to walk this journey of preparation and stewardship. May this book become a tool of peace and wisdom in your hands.

Finally, I am grateful to the Most High, the force behind the divine avalanche, the very air that I breathe, the summit of all things beautiful in my life, for being not only the source of every provision entrusted to me but also the patient teacher who reveals how blessing must be transformed to give life. For the snowfields are his, yet so too is the wisdom that melts the snow into meltwater. I am grateful for his guidance, for the unseen instruction by which provision becomes nourishment, and for trusting me to remain a vessel in his hands, that what he sends may not rest frozen in my possession but flow outward to further his kingdom and bless others, many of whom I will never meet.

DISCLAIMER:

This book was written out of prayer, study, reflection, and personal experience. Any true insight belongs to the Lord; any mistakes are my own. The ideas, prayers, and discernment expressed in these pages were formed in God's presence and through lived experience.

In the preparation of this work, I made limited use of contemporary writing and language tools, including AI-assisted editing technologies. This limited and supervised use accords with the Church's guidance on emerging technology. In *Magnifica Humanitas* (2026), Pope Leo XIV's encyclical on safeguarding the human person in the time of artificial intelligence, Pope Leo characterizes such technology as "a valuable tool that requires vigilance" to prevent it from dominating humanity. Left unchecked, such tools become a kind of master; rightly ordered, they serve the common good. In that same spirit, these tools were used solely for the purpose of language refinement, such as clarity, tone, structure, and grammatical correction, helping to express my original thoughts in a more readable and pastoral form. No theological concepts, core frameworks, or governing ideas originated from these systems. The underlying perspectives, interpretations, insights, and spiritual impressions contained herein arise from prayer, contemplation, research, and personal discernment.

Avalanche theology is presented, branded, and legally protected as *God's Divine Avalanche*™ for purposes of authorship and clarity. Yet the author acknowledges it as belonging ultimately to God alone. The framework is not claimed as an invention, but understood as the fruit of prayer, reflection, and contemplation before the Lord. This entire work is a received understanding rather than a created system. To God alone belongs the credit for any truth, coherence, or benefit that may be found within these pages.

All product names, logos, and brands are property of their respective owners. Use of these names does not imply endorsement. Website links, online platforms, and parish structures referenced in this book were accurate at the time of writing but may change, expire, or become unavailable after publication. The author assumes no responsibility for links that no longer function, or for the content, accuracy, or availability of any third-party website referenced herein.

The material presented here addresses financial habits, emotional stewardship, discipline, accountability, and values alignment. It is offered as a type of pastoral-psychological articulation of theological anthropology for educational and spiritual formation purposes only and should not be construed as financial, legal, tax, or investment advice. Please consult a qualified, licensed financial professional before making financial decisions. The author and publisher are not responsible for how readers choose to apply this material.

Where historical or cultural background is discussed, I have relied primarily on biblical and Catholic reference works, together with carefully selected secular sources, to ensure accuracy and clarity.

The primary sources informing this work are Sacred Scripture, the Catechism of the Catholic Church, the writings of the Church Fathers, the witness of the saints, and the teaching of the papal magisterium. These sources, many of which are available online, provide the theological foundation and interpretive framework of the book. Secondary sources serve a supportive role, edifying rather than governing the theological argument. References to modern psychology, behavioral economics, and human behavior research serve as illuminating tools rather than authorities on doctrine, offering insight into the mechanisms of perception, attachment, decision, and transformation that the spiritual tradition has long observed. Lastly, to deepen and enrich the central metaphor, a range of scientific references on avalanche formation and behavior were also consulted, allowing the natural dynamics of snow accumulation, release, and flow to more faithfully reflect the spiritual truths explored in this work.

It is my hope that you will come away from this book sensing a harmony rather than a tension: a work that is deeply rooted in Catholic thought, yet intellectually attentive to the patterns of human experience. Readers who wish to explore these themes more fully are encouraged to consult the bibliography provided at the end of the book.

My sincere desire is that every word here leads you not to human opinion, but deeper into trust in God's wisdom and care. These reflections are offered as invitations to prayer, discernment, and personal contemplation; but no book, no framework, no human language can substitute for the living guidance of God. At best, these words may help illuminate or encourage—they are never intended to replace the quiet work of divine instruction from God himself.

If anything within these pages bears fruit, may it deepen peace, strengthen discernment, and draw the reader toward greater confidence in the Lord's providence. If anything falls short, may it be set aside without hesitation.

TABLE OF CONTENTS

Prologue

Today in America, there are hundreds, if not thousands, of books about building wealth through hard work, saving, and long-term investing.

This is not one of them.

This book wrestles with what psychotherapists call "Sudden Wealth Syndrome," a term coined by wealth psychologists Stephen Goldbart and Joan DiFuria at their Money, Meaning & Choices Institute to describe the emotional and cognitive turbulence that some people experience after coming into a large amount of money faster than the mind and heart can absorb. Sudden Wealth Syndrome does not mean something is inherently wrong with a person. It means the whole person is scrambling to adjust to a dramatic event. In other words, it describes what happens when blessing arrives faster than formation.

Sudden wealth can feel like the emotional whiplash of an avalanche: powerful, disorienting, and demanding decisions that must be made quickly, before the soul is ready. Anxiety and fear may rise.

"What if I lose it?"

"Who can I trust?"

Guilt or a sense of unworthiness quickly follows, especially when others around them are struggling themselves. Some feel ashamed, worried that people will judge them or treat them differently, and they begin to withdraw, creating isolation to avoid pressure or conflict. Decision-making can freeze, as they become afraid to spend or invest, afraid even to touch the money. Others swing in the opposite direction, overspending, giving impulsively, or making risky financial choices. Relationships may strain under new expectations and requests. Jealousy seeps in, or disappointment rises when answers do not come swiftly. Beneath it all, many wrestle with identity confusion, wondering who they are now and what their life is supposed to look like in light of this sudden change.

If you have never experienced something like this, you may wonder: "How does anyone really come into wealth overnight, and why would it be so hard to handle?"

Observe the following examples:

1) A content creator, author, or artist goes viral.
2) A student-athlete secures an NIL contract.
3) A tech startup becomes a unicorn.
4) An heir inherits a large estate.
5) A real estate valuation surges.
6) A digital coin appreciates exponentially.
7) An actor lands a major leading role.
8) An executive is recruited to the C-suite of a Fortune 500 company.
9) An investment skyrockets overnight.
10) A retail worker wins a large lottery jackpot.

Take the last example. Millions buy lottery tickets every year, imagining life transformed overnight. Yet the reality is sobering. A widely cited figure—one that appears in a report on the American Bankruptcy Institute's website—holds that nearly one-third of lottery winners in the United States declare bankruptcy within three to five years of their windfall. The underlying data is debated, but the message is consistent: sudden wealth can leave winners worse off than they were before they won. (A brief word here, since the lottery will surface again in these pages: some Christians consider playing it inherently sinful. The Catholic tradition is more measured. The Catechism teaches that games of chance "are not in themselves contrary to justice," but become morally unacceptable when they deprive a person of what is needed to provide for himself and others, or when "the passion for gambling risks becoming an enslavement" (CCC 2413). Like wealth itself, the lottery is not evil in its essence; the danger lies in disordered desire. I reference it not to commend or condemn it, but because, like any sudden windfall, it reveals what is already in the heart that receives it.) But it is not just lottery winners who are vulnerable. Many who experience sudden wealth face unique perils. Even among the ultra-wealthy, not all fortunes are self-made. Drawing on the Forbes World's Billionaires List, one 2025 analysis found that of roughly 2,800 billionaires worldwide, about 67 percent are self-made while 33 percent inherited their wealth.

Why mention this at all? Because it underscores a powerful truth: whether riches come by windfall, entrepreneurship, or inheritance, preparation is the difference between blessing and bondage.

To be clear, this book is not about tech startup valuations or lottery jackpots. It is about something far greater: *God's divine avalanche.* Unlike chance winnings or overnight success, God's blessings come with purpose and call us into something larger than ourselves.

While sudden abundance often captures attention, this book moves beyond the work of psychologists and therapists who have popularized the term Sudden Wealth Syndrome. Their insights help illuminate the emotional turbulence that can accompany rapid financial change, offering helpful frameworks such as "affluence IQ" and providing a valuable foundation for understanding these challenges. These realities remain strikingly relevant and continue to affect many followers of Jesus Christ. However, the aim of this book is to map the terrain of spiritual formation surrounding sudden wealth. Without the spiritual, relational, and financial groundwork that Scripture reveals and God intends, sudden riches can overwhelm—or even bury—the unprepared.

Now pause for a moment. Is this another book preaching the virtues of a prosperity gospel?

Not at all. The prosperity gospel is the belief that God promises financial wealth, physical health, and success in return for faith, positive confession, or specific acts of obedience. This book, however, is about spiritual formation, about the readiness into which disciples of

Jesus Christ are called so that sudden abundance may be received as life-giving rather than overwhelming. Without wisdom and preparation, even God-ordained increase can crush rather than nurture.

This book does something rare: it takes wealthy people seriously as souls who need formation, not just management. That conviction runs through every page that follows. When priorities are disordered, even a blessing can become a burden. Readiness allows sudden provision to be received as nourishment rather than strain. And, quite frankly, human history, including biblical history, is full of moments where gifts intended for good were mishandled, misunderstood, or misused.

You may still ask, "Won't God send the rain, the snow, or the harvest to a disorganized person anyway?" My response is a confident *yes*. Scripture affirms that God, in his sovereignty, sends rain on both the just and the unjust. But Scripture also shows that while God gives rain freely, he does not promise that everyone will be able to receive it well. Rain or snow that falls on unprepared ground can become runoff or erosion rather than nourishment. In the same way, blessing given without formation may arrive by grace… but it is stewardship that determines whether it bears fruit or washes away.

Provision itself is not a measure of virtue. Yet the Spirit continually calls us into a life shaped by wisdom so that we can experience a life filled with joy that endures. The urgency for followers of Christ, then, is not to control the rain or the snowfall—that remains God's domain—but to order our hearts rightly so that what God sends may be received as blessing rather than experienced as burden. That is precisely how this book was born. It did not begin in a library or a seminar. It began in a sacred space.

MY TESTIMONY

I was born and raised in the Roman Catholic Church, the daughter of Cuban exiles who had fled Castro's regime and rebuilt their lives in New York and Miami. But like many, I wandered off in college—chasing degrees, ambitions, and a life that felt a little more in step with an '80s girl at NYU. Catholicism, at the time, seemed too quiet, too ancient, and far less interesting than pop culture, late nights, and the creative chaos of filmmakers, artists, and writers.

One summer break, I returned to Miami and wandered into a bookstore in South Miami. I picked up Mother Teresa's autobiography and opened it at random to a chapter on holiness. The first line stopped me: "Holiness is not the luxury of a few. It is everyone's duty: yours and mine." I did not put the book down until I had finished it. Not long after, alone in my bedroom, I gave my life to God. What followed was unlike anything I had words for… a presence that entered the room and seemed to pin me to my bed, a stillness so weighty I could not move. I would later come to understand the distinction the mystics make between the anointing of the Spirit, which empowers movement, and the glory of God, which can arrest it entirely. That night, I encountered the latter.

What followed was forty years of walking with God as a proud and, admittedly at times, lukewarm Protestant.

It was the faith in which I married my husband, raised my sons, and navigated some of the most difficult seasons of my life. Although far from fully matured as a Christian, God was always at work during those years. We must not cast our eyes downward upon our wilderness seasons. The desert is rarely wasted ground. More often, desert formation is where God does his most decisive and transformative work—forging the soul long before we recognize what he is preparing us to receive.

I began to find my way back to the Catholic Church almost unexpectedly, through a classmate at Fuller who introduced me to the writings of Henri Nouwen. What began as an academic encounter gradually became something far more personal.

As a Protestant, I often felt as though I were drifting across a vast ocean in a small paddleboat—moving forward, yes, but largely on my own strength. Occasionally, I would meet another believer, and we would tie our boats together for a time, sharing direction and encouragement. But eventually, the currents would separate us, and I would find myself alone again, paddling through open water.

Catholicism has felt entirely different. It is as though I have been pulled aboard a great ship, one that has been crossing these waters for centuries. There are hands to help, voices to guide, and a sense that I am no longer navigating alone, but being carried within something far larger and steadier than myself.

Slowly, I came to see that in the Catholic Church, God has already done much of the heavy lifting, establishing a sacramental life, a priesthood, and a living communion of believers that surrounds and sustains the faithful. Through the intercession of the Blessed Mother and the saints, and the steady life of the Church itself, I began to experience something I never had before—a sense that heaven itself has my back. For someone shaped by achievement, this realization was both disarming and freeing. I was no longer carrying my spiritual life alone but learning to receive it within a communion that prays, intercedes, and walks with me. For someone so accustomed to striving, that realization changed everything.

Amid a long and often painful journey of self-discovery (what I now think of as my "wooing season"), I did not expect to fall so deeply in love with the living presence of Christ in the Eucharist. And yet, that is exactly what happened, and why I adopted St. Carlo Acutis as my patron saint. It was there, in the stillness of the Adoration Chapel at Queen of Peace, that my faith deepened in a way I could not have planned or produced. It was no longer sustained by words, or teaching, or even religion alone… but by presence.

One afternoon, as I knelt before the Blessed Sacrament, overwhelmed and crying out to the Lord, I was suddenly given an image: an avalanche, roaring down a mountain with terrifying force. Startled, I dismissed it at once. I assumed it was a distraction, perhaps even a temptation meant to pull my focus away from God at a moment of intimacy and surrender.

But the image returned.

This time, the scene changed. Winter gave way to spring. The snow that had thundered down the mountainside began to melt, feeding rivers and streams, filling lakes and valleys with life below. What had first appeared destructive was now revealed as nourishment flowing where it was most needed.

I left the chapel unsettled, but attentive. As I turned to Scripture, the meaning slowly unfolded. The avalanche was not an apocalyptic vision, nor a warning, nor a temptation. It was an invitation. The Lord was showing me that sudden abundance, especially financial provision, could either overwhelm or sustain, depending on whether one was prepared to steward it.

He was calling me to *readiness.*

Over the next four months, I returned to the Word, cross-referencing every passage I could find that spoke of sudden wealth or sudden abundance, using the New Oxford Annotated Bible, a widely used ecumenical study Bible common in seminaries and academic settings. What emerged was not a scholarly treatise or academic argument, but something far more personal: the outline of a small, meditative book, one I could carry with me, tucked into my tote bag, ready to open whenever I felt the pull to return to the Adoration Chapel and sit again before the Lord.

God's Divine Avalanche was born not out of ambition, but out of prayer, Scripture, and a call to prepare for what God might desire to release, not only in my life, but in the lives of those willing to receive his abundance with discretion and care.

And yet, even while I was preparing and obeying as I believed the Lord had asked me to do, the doubts persisted. Over and over I wondered, "Is God sending me a financial avalanche? Is that what all this means? But how? I am not even tithing." Another question followed close behind: "Could God have meant something broader than finances?" Possibly. But the image that kept returning—snow melting into streams of provision, and the peace that followed—seemed to point toward financial stewardship.

And the confirmation I sensed repeatedly was simple and consistent, that I need to prepare. I needed to confront the disordered priorities rooted in fear and anxiety, and trust that he would show me how. I began with a small, stapled stack of pages—familiar verses gathered, prayed over, and carried with me into the quiet of Adoration. As those verses began to grow into stories that shaped my own formation, I did what I often do with good news from God: I shared it. I self-published a handful of paperback, pocket-sized copies to give to friends and family. They were never meant to persuade or convince, but to accompany prayer and spark conversation, small enough to hold, to return to, to keep close. I resisted the urge to proclaim what my heart longs to believe: "Yes! Sudden abundance is coming for you, too. Get ready."

But abundance, whether sudden or gradual, belongs to God alone. We cannot claim that careful preparation guarantees the release of a divine avalanche, as though order itself compels provision. That is a false premise. We prepare not to force God's hand but to be ready, so that if sudden abundance arrives, it can be received with wisdom rather than fear.

It is my sincere hope that God's provision would touch every household, including yours. Yet that hope is not the prayer of this book, nor its calling. The purpose here is not to promise sudden abundance, but to prepare your heart for it. When God chooses to release his provision, like snow released from the mountain, it must be stewarded with care so that it yields life beyond a single moment. When received with wisdom, sudden provision becomes a living river, carrying life into families, resilience into communities, and continuity into generations. When received without preparation, the same provision can destabilize, scatter, and disappear, flowing outward until nothing remains but traces left far from the mountain that birthed it.

Some readers may hesitate here, and rightly so. Many have been wounded by teachings that equated wealth with faithfulness and suffering with failure. Those messages have left behind shame, confusion, and spiritual exhaustion. God's divine avalanche is not a promise of riches or a formula for financial gain. Hebrews 11 teaches us that many of the faithful never saw material increase in their lifetime, yet God called them victorious. Their reward was deeper trust, not sudden wealth.

> *"All of these died in faith without having received the promises, but from a distance they saw and greeted them…."*
> HEBREWS 11:13

Rather, this book is a pilgrimage, a call to discernment and spiritual formation through a pastoral, psychological, and theo-anthropological lens. It is an invitation to prepare the heart, habits, and hands for whatever God may entrust, whether much or little. It is written especially for those who find themselves caught unprepared by sudden wealth, for men and women who did not seek abundance, did not plan for it, and yet find themselves suddenly entrusted with more than they know how to hold. It is also written for those who once held such abundance and watched it slip through their hands, still wondering what happened to the resources that were once entrusted to them.

For some, the image of an avalanche may resonate deeply… as metaphor, as intuition, or even as a personal spiritual impression. However it appears, the invitation remains the same: readiness. Abundance is not measured by excess but by readiness. It is the capacity to receive without distortion and to steward without being consumed. The question is not whether God can bring sudden provision, but whether you are prepared if he does.

A WORD OF CAUTION

I am fully aware that many people today do not have time to read. Some of you may be tempted to jump straight to Chapter 6 (the heart work) or to the practical readiness of Chapter 7 because life is pulling you in several directions and time feels scarce. And perhaps, if we are being honest, you simply want the practical guidance. You may feel weary of spiritual language that sounds preachy or familiar, like something you have already heard from the pulpit on any given Sunday. I understand that impulse; but I want to offer a gentle word of caution.

If you apply the practical application exercises without first cultivating a supportive inner environment, or without honestly engaging the deeper issues explored, you may experience short-term relief, but not lasting change. You might stabilize your circumstances for a season, only to find yourself repeating familiar patterns later on. This is because change is not sustained by technique alone. It requires understanding. It requires formation, and formation does not unfold through shortcuts or simple formulas. Formation is slow, demanding, and often uncomfortable. It asks us to look back with honesty, to examine the decisions we made, the voices we trusted, and the paths we followed, and to acknowledge that not all of them were good, stable, or life-giving. As we grow older, this kind of reflection often becomes harder, not easier. Our habits become settled, our explanations for the past become familiar, and it can be unsettling to revisit the influences that shaped our choices. Yet it is only through such honest examination that authentic transformation becomes possible.

HOW TO ENGAGE THIS JOURNEY

Throughout this book you will encounter more than ideas. Some chapters include guided prayers, reflective prompts, cognitive exercises, and/or practical applications. Each phase of the divine avalanche concludes with a case study built around a modern fictional character inspired by the Apostle John—recognized as the disciple whom Christ loved, and one whose identity was firmly rooted as a child of God. At the foot of the cross, John received a profound gift when Jesus said, "Behold, your mother" (John 19:27). In that moment, John became more than a disciple; he became a representative of all who would come to follow Christ, entrusted with Mary not only as his mother, but as a spiritual mother to all believers. In this way, John stands as a symbol of every soul who receives both identity and belonging through Christ: adopted, loved, and formed within a living spiritual family. Hence, Johnny Beloved was created to help translate insight into lived formation.

These elements are not techniques to master, but invitations to participate. Spiritual and interior change rarely comes through information alone. True understanding grows when we give ourselves time to pause, reflect, and carefully align our lives with what we are learning. As you read, you may find it helpful to move slowly, allowing space not only to absorb the words but also to notice what stirs your attention and invites deeper reflection. You might consider using a yellow highlighter to mark words or phrases that stand out to you. If you are Catholic, you may also wish to prayerfully sit with those words through *lectio divina*, allowing the Holy Spirit to speak through them in a personal way. There is no requirement to complete every exercise, nor any pressure to progress at a particular pace. Formation is not mechanical. Engage what resonates, return to what unsettles, and allow the process to unfold with patience.

You may find it helpful to read this book more than once. Formation rarely unfolds in a single pass. Human fears, attachments, wounds, assumptions, and long-established patterns tend to surface gradually. Each encounter with an idea can reveal something new, not because the words have changed but because the reader has. Grace often works in this layered, progressive manner. What feels merely interesting on a first reading may feel deeply personal on a second and clarifying on a third.

Think of the journey this way…

❄ First reading: awakening and recognition

❄ Second reading: reflection and realignment

❄ Third reading: integration and readiness

If you truly desire lasting change, resist the urge to rush.

Let the snow build. The order matters.

Introduction
GOD'S DIVINE AVALANCHE (AIPOM)

In the natural world, an avalanche is both terrifying and majestic. It begins in what is called the *start zone*, high on the mountain, where layers of snow have been slowly building over time—unseen, silent, and patient. The mountain can appear completely still just moments before it moves. Then suddenly, under the right conditions, a hidden layer gives way, and the snow races downward with unstoppable force.

While there are several types of avalanches, for the purpose of this metaphor we will focus on the power of a slab release—though what you may picture resembles the sweeping, billowing movement of a powder avalanche. As described by Bruce Tremper in *Staying Alive in Avalanche Terrain*, these releases occur where gradual buildup meets instability, where slope steepness, accumulated load, structural weakness, and a trigger all converge. In fact, many avalanches begin partway down the mountain. They do not always start at the summit, but at the point where instability meets accumulation. For the sake of this metaphor, however, we will hold that definition loosely and imagine an avalanche beginning at the top, pouring down a defined path into the valley below with great force. Like all metaphors, this one has limits. Certain elements, such as the runoff and erosion that can occur, will be addressed more directly as we move forward.

To those in its path, an avalanche can be destructive and overwhelming. People and animals can be swept off their feet, buried beneath tons of snow, and suffocated within minutes. But scientists have observed that avalanches damage far more than the narrow chute of snow itself. According to the U.S. Geological Survey, the force they generate creates a powerful air blast that can flatten trees, collapse structures, and injure or kill even those standing outside the direct path. As the moving snow accelerates, it tears loose everything in its way—trees, rocks, fences, and debris—and hurls them downslope with violent speed, multiplying the destruction. The Colorado Avalanche Information Center (CAIC) in Boulder, Colorado, notes that avalanches are not just dramatic winter events; they are the most dangerous natural hazard the state faces. More lives have been lost to avalanches there than to any other kind of natural disaster, reminding us just how powerful and unpredictable they can be.

Yet researchers explain that within the larger rhythm of creation, the avalanche also serves a vital, ecosystemic purpose. Avalanches tend to follow long-established paths, rarely carving new ones. When the snow finally settles and melts, it feeds the valleys, rivers, and streams, carrying soil, broken branches, and nutrients that enrich the land below. Even the scars left behind become places where new forests eventually take root.

What looks like destruction in the moment often becomes provision in time.

And so it is in the spiritual realm—at least it was in my situation. When God showed me an avalanche in a vision, it was not simply about destruction or fear. It was a simple metaphor of sudden release. Not a reward finally tallied, but a readiness finally formed. For years, prayer, faith, obedience, perseverance, and even redemptive suffering had been doing their quiet work—not filling a reservoir until God was compelled to act, but shaping a soul until it could bear what God had always intended to give. Like snow building on a mountaintop, the formation happens mostly out of sight. And then, in God's timing, what has been accumulating is released. What follows is an outpouring the soul could not have received any earlier, and could not have survived without the years that came before.

For some, the word *sudden* evokes anxiety. For others, the avalanche signifies long-awaited relief… an answer to long-held prayers for provision, opened doors, released burdens, or new streams of opportunity. In such moments, it may feel as though God is responding to cries carried silently for years.

Yet even blessings can unsettle. With great outpouring comes both promise and peril, the enduring paradox of abundance. Like snow rushing down a mountain, money can nourish or destroy. It can refresh the land or bury the unprepared. Perhaps you have already known such a season: an inheritance, an opportunity, a financial turning point that arrived unexpectedly, only for it to slip away despite your best intentions. As a result, you may ask, "Why does abundance often prove difficult not only to attain, but to sustain?"

Sudden provision can be as disorienting as it is extraordinary. When resources arrive before understanding, stability, or inner readiness, they may produce pressure rather than peace, confusion rather than clarity. What appears as blessing can become weight when the structures to hold it are not yet formed.

Through Scripture, reflection, and lived insight, this book explores the relationship between provision and formation, inviting readers to consider how *identity, discernment*, and *stewardship* shape the impact of sudden abundance. Perhaps your encounter with this book is itself a form of preparation, an invitation to understand both the promise and the danger of sudden increase.

Just as wise mountaineers respect the mountain, we too must respect the avalanche of blessing.

Not resisting it.

Not fearing it.

But preparing our hearts, our homes, and our lives to channel it into rivers of life.

If you sense a calling to steward wealth—to ready your spirit, mind, and hands for both the weight of provision and the responsibility it carries—then welcome to the lessons of God's divine avalanche. What follows is the ancient pattern Scripture traces for every soul called to receive what God has been building toward.

YOUR PILGRIMAGE MAP: AIPOM

The biblical account is the story of God's relentless love for humanity, yet it also reveals the terrain of that love—mountains climbed, deserts crossed, covenants sealed, failures redeemed, and abundance entrusted. But the Bible is not only a love story; it is also a map. Not a roadmap, which is an engineered journey, but a navigational map. An engineered journey assumes the path can be designed in advance, outcomes are predictable, progress is linear, control is central, and technique produces results. It is the mindset behind business plans, productivity systems, self-help formulas, optimization culture, and twelve-step programs. Rather, a navigated journey assumes that the terrain exists before the traveler, that conditions can change at any moment, and that control is limited. Discernment is essential when movement requires this level of awareness.

You do not build the world; you move through it.

This is how sailors travel, pilgrims move, explorers survive, humans actually live, and biblical figures walk with God. From Genesis to Revelation, God does not merely reveal who he is; he unveils how he and his people move toward one another. He moves first, disclosing not only his nature, but his way—how he forms, how he leads, how blessing unfolds through history. Scripture traces a consistent pattern: calling before commissioning, belonging before inheritance, formation before fruitfulness. God does not act randomly. He acts deliberately and patiently. Then we respond, not by moving around his mysteries, but by moving through them.

This is how the biblical story unfolds, as a living, faithful, and sometimes stubborn journey told over generations. God never asks his people to wander blindly. He provides direction, rhythm, and structure for transformation, leading his people not only toward promise but toward the kind of heart capable of receiving it. The divine avalanche follows such a pattern, and throughout Scripture this pattern repeats:

God grants *access* through covenant.

He establishes *identity* before inheritance.

He allows *preparation* to accumulate over time.

He reveals *opportunity* when the heart is formed and ready.

And in his timing, he releases *multiplication* that flows outward, nourishing many.

This pilgrimage can be remembered through the map I call... **AIPOM:**

A—Access
I—Identity
P—Preparation
O—Opportunity
M—Multiplication

Looking at AIPOM as five equal steps or beats misses the most important feature of the map: it is not symmetrical. The first three stages—Access, Identity, Preparation—are the work of years. They unfold beneath the surface, in interior places no one can see, often without any sign that something is happening at all. The last two, Opportunity and Multiplication, are the work of moments. They arrive with a force that feels disproportionate to the time leading up to them.

God reveals divine order without promising instant results. Snow accumulates patiently across a long winter. One day, seemingly out of nowhere, the mountain releases it in seconds. This is the shape of the avalanche, and the shape of God's work in a faithful life. It guards us from both despair and pride, from assuming we are forgotten when nothing seems to move, and from claiming credit when blessing finally arrives. What looks like sudden grace is almost always the long work of God beneath the surface.

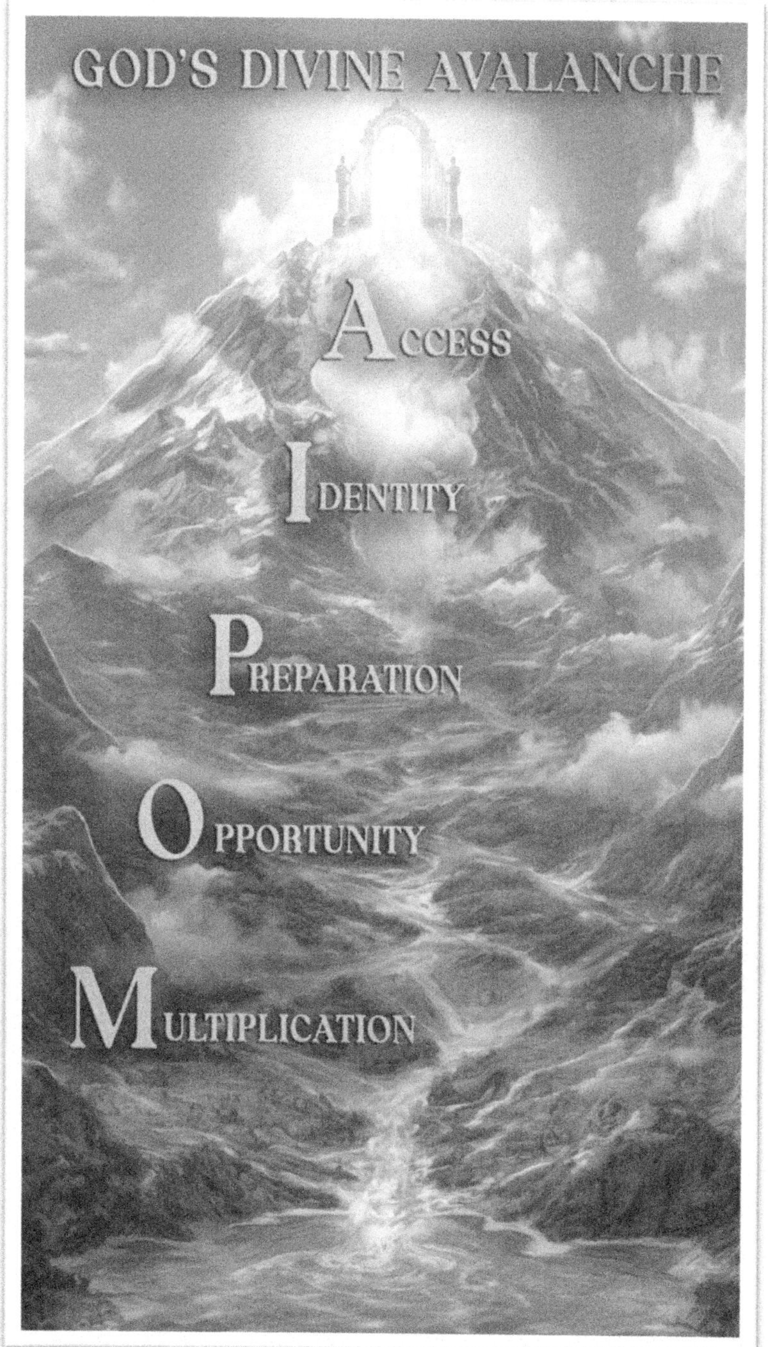
GOD'S DIVINE AVALANCHE
ACCESS
IDENTITY
PREPARATION
OPPORTUNITY
MULTIPLICATION

1

From Map to Movement: The Divine Avalanche as a Cycle

A map alone is not enough. A map tells you where you are. It does not show you what it feels like when the terrain begins to move beneath your feet.

The divine avalanche is that movement.

What AIPOM describes in structure, the divine avalanche reveals in motion. What appears as sudden release is not random; it follows a pattern, the same pattern Scripture reveals, and the same pattern AIPOM names.

The divine avalanche, then, is not separate from the map. *It is the map in motion.*

The Divine Avalanche as a Cycle

In nature, avalanches may seem like isolated events, but what crashes down the mountain often does not disappear. Over time, the snow settles and melts, seeping into the ground to feed rivers and streams that water the valley and sustain life far beyond where it first fell. This may feel like destruction, but it is not.

This is a system—God's enduring pattern of provision.

In the same way, financial blessings are not meant to end with us. They belong to a larger movement of grace, flowing outward to nourish families and communities, reaching forward into generations to come. Creation itself teaches this cycle. When we begin to recognize it, we step into a new role—not just as receivers of blessing, but as *channels of blessing.*

Here is how the inner work of AIPOM meets the outer movement of the cycle:

- ❄ Access is the *Pre-Snow Phase*, where positioning happens before any snow can fall.
- ❄ Identity is the *Temperature Drop Phase,* where the inner conditions of the heart prepare to receive what is coming.
- ❄ Preparation spans both the *Snowfields* and the *Avalanche* itself, the long accumulation of formation and the moment when, in God's timing, the snow breaks free.
- ❄ Opportunity is the *Meltwater Phase*, where what has fallen begins to transform into something the soul can hold.
- ❄ And Multiplication unfolds across the *Rivers* and the *Valley*, as blessing flows outward and embeds itself in generations.

Taken together, AIPOM is one continuous movement from the unseen work of the soul to the lives the blessing will reach.

I. SETTING THE CONDITIONS: *Pre-Snow and Temperature Drop Phases*

Before a single layer of snow can accumulate, the mountain must first be prepared. The conditions must change. The temperature must drop. The environment must become receptive to what is about to form. Without this unseen shift, no snow will remain, and no avalanche can ever occur.

So it is in the life of faith. Access places us on the mountain—the invitation into God's provision and purpose. From this starting point, identity establishes the conditions of the heart, creating the internal alignment that allows what God sends to remain. Before anything accumulates, before anything is released, the soul must be positioned and formed to receive.

Every movement of blessing begins here, in what is unseen and often overlooked.

II. The Snowfields: *Accumulation of Formation*

Most avalanches begin with snow at the heights. Long before movement, long before the thunderous descent, the mountain gathers what will one day be released, far above where anyone is watching. Layer upon layer, the snowfields grow with the slow labor of faithfulness and obedience.

> *"I lift up my eyes to the hills—from where will my help come? My help comes from the Lord, who made heaven and earth."*
> Psalm 121:1–2

Every blessing we encounter in life ultimately originates in God. We are not the source—only the stewards. This truth both humbles and liberates us. We do not create the mountain, nor do we command the seasons that gather the snow. Provision often exists long before it becomes visible to us, shaped by conditions and purposes beyond our immediate understanding.

Yet while we are not the authors of blessing, we are not passive within it. The snowfields of formation accumulate through lived participation—through faithfulness held over time, through obedience that becomes second nature, through trust that sticks when nothing visible justifies it. We do not manufacture provision, but we do cooperate with grace, preparing the ground upon which blessing may one day settle.

Because of this, we need not strive to force blessing into existence, nor cling to it as though it were ours alone to secure. What God entrusts is meant to be received with gratitude and guided with wisdom, always remembering the one from whom it came.

III. THE AVALANCHE: *Sudden Release*

When the snow breaks free, it represents the sudden outpouring of God's provision. It can be dramatic, even overwhelming. The scale alone may exceed what we can take in all at once.

> *"[A]nd thus put me to the test, says the Lord of hosts; see if I will not open the windows of heaven for you and pour down for you an overflowing blessing."*
> MALACHI 3:10

Blessings are not always gradual. Sometimes God releases abundance all at once, and when he does, the gift carries weight. Provision that arrives suddenly does not instantly become life-giving. Like snow freshly fallen, it possesses immense potential, but it must settle and take shape before it becomes something the soul can hold.

Snow alone does not break loose into an avalanche. The release comes from the interaction of layers, temperature, and wind—and shifting conditions beyond our sight. Snow may sit for long periods without movement, while subtle, unseen changes prepare the moment of release. Stability has more to do with structure and environment than with quantity.

Blessing often follows a similar mystery. Accumulation may be present long before movement. Release may depend on conditions beyond human perception. For this reason, sudden provision asks for preparation—wisdom in hand and humility in heart—so that what falls upon us does not bury us. Instead, it must become something we can faithfully steward and eventually channel.

IV. The Meltwater: *Transformation of Blessing*

As the avalanche settles and melts with the rise of temperatures, the snow becomes flexible, usable, life-giving water. Here, provision begins its second work—no longer arriving, but being shaped: into investments, into generosity, into the kind of security that outlasts the one who built it.

> *"For as the rain and the snow come down from heaven, and do not return there until they have watered the earth, making it bring forth and sprout, giving seed to the sower and bread to the eater…."*
>
> Isaiah 55:10

Just as snow alone cannot nourish the earth while frozen, financial provision alone does not automatically produce life. Snow may be abundant, even breathtaking in its scale, yet while locked in its frozen state it cannot hydrate the soil that needs it. Only when it melts, when its form changes, does it become life-giving.

Provision follows the same law. The presence of something is not the same as the benefit of something. One may possess great provision while remaining profoundly unnourished.

We see this pattern everywhere:

- ❄ Someone with wealth, yet burdened by constant anxiety.
- ❄ A student surrounded by courses, yet lacking understanding.
- ❄ A person immersed in relationships, yet experiencing loneliness.
- ❄ An abundance of information that generates noise rather than clarity.
- ❄ A life full of activity, yet lacking direction or purpose.

In each case, provision exists, yet nourishment is absent. This recognition reveals a deeper truth: resources alone do not guarantee life-giving impact. External inputs are not automatically transformative. Snow that never melts cannot sustain life. Provision that is never transformed cannot nourish. Nourishment occurs only when what is received becomes metabolized, ordered, and directed toward living systems:

- ❄ Food nourishes when it is absorbed by the body.
- ❄ Money nourishes when it reduces instability or enables purpose.

- ❄ Education nourishes when it reshapes perception and capacity.
- ❄ Information nourishes when it clarifies rather than overwhelms.
- ❄ Relationships nourish when they strengthen the inner life.

Nourishment always answers a single question: Does this genuinely support life? Provision asks only whether something has arrived. For this reason, stewardship is more than the management of resources. It is the facilitation of transformation itself. The calling reaches beyond receiving. It is participation in the melting, guiding blessings from frozen potential into living impact.

Whenever provision enters our lives, wisdom invites us to stop and examine our position honestly:

- ❄ Is this merely present, or is it beneficial?
- ❄ Does this sustain, or simply exist?
- ❄ Does this reduce friction, or generate noise?
- ❄ Does this deepen life, or merely decorate it?

V. THE RIVERS: *Flow to Others*

Once snow has melted, and once provision has been transformed into life-giving substance, it continues its journey. The water gathers and begins to flow, forming rivers that carry nourishment far beyond their point of origin. Meltwater that does not move cannot stay life-giving for long. Left standing, it stagnates. Only in motion does water nourish the land it touches and the life that depends on it downstream.

Blessing follows the same design. What has been transformed into nourishment is meant to move outward, carried into places where life can grow.

God's provision, once made life-giving, naturally seeks movement. It is carried outward into places where it can restore what is lacking and bring increase. The purpose of blessing is not fulfilled in storage. It is fulfilled in circulation.

> *"[A]nd let the one who believes in me drink. As the scripture has said, 'Out of the believer's heart shall flow rivers of living water.'"*
> JOHN 7:38

The true measure of stewardship, therefore, is how faithfully nourishment is allowed to flow. Wise preservation matters.

Blessing hoarded in fear becomes anxiety.

Blessing released without wisdom dissipates.

But blessing directed in alignment with purpose becomes generative, renewing both giver and receiver.

When nourishment flows outward, it becomes more than possession; it becomes healing where there was strain, provision where there was lack, stability where there was uncertainty, and faith where there was doubt. What began as God's gift to one life becomes God's care to many.

VI. THE VALLEY: *Generational and Communal Nourishment*

Eventually, the rivers reach the valley. This is the final intended destination—the low place where water finishes its work. Here, nourishment is no longer merely flowing; it becomes embedded. Soil is softened. Seeds take root. Fields are cultivated. Communities rise. Life organizes itself around what the rivers sustain. The valley is where provision, having been transformed and carried, becomes generative. What began as distant snow now supports harvests, and what once fell in sudden abundance becomes stability and lasting growth. The drama of the avalanche disappears, yet its effects endure everywhere. Nourishment becomes so integrated into life that its origin is easily forgotten.

> *"I will make of you a great nation, and I will bless you, and make your name great, so that you will be a blessing."*
> Genesis 12:2

This is the long reach of blessing, the stage at which God's provision outlives the moment of its arrival and even the lifetime of its receiver. In the valley, blessing ceases to be an event and becomes an environment. Here, nourishment produces what isolated provision never could. Households are sustained rather than merely relieved. Structures rise that outlast the transactions that built them. Security takes root, and futures begin to form that we may never live to see.

Your blessing, therefore, is not designed to terminate at your household. It is meant to participate in systems of life that are spiritual and practical, that extend beyond your sight and beyond your years. For the valley is the geography of legacy. When God entrusts abundance, he often operates with generational horizons. What we experience as personal provision may, in his design, be seed for lives we will never witness. Blessing that reaches this stage shapes whole civilizations across generations.

THE RUNOFF: *When Blessing Escapes Its Intended Purpose*

In creation, not all meltwater remains within the life-giving system of rivers and valleys. Some water rushes beyond its natural boundaries, carried away to the ocean, where it no longer nourishes the mountain's ecosystem. Though not wasted in an absolute sense, it no longer serves the land from which it came.

Financial blessing can behave the same way. When increase comes without vision or stewardship to anchor it, the money tends to flow right back out before it has time to build anything. No stability forms. No legacy takes shape. Resources that could have strengthened a household or seeded something for the next generation get spent on impulse or absorbed by everyday consumption. What is left often funnels into systems that have no covenantal tie to the person who earned it—markets, institutions, tax authorities, distant economies, sometimes even strangers. They all benefit. Meanwhile, the giver's own family and community, and the inheritance that was supposed to outlast them, see very little of the provision that once passed through their hands. The tragedy of the runoff is not that blessing flowed. The tragedy is that it never settled long enough to nourish what it was entrusted to sustain. Stewardship is more than letting blessing flow. It is choosing where it lands and takes root.

CLOSING REFLECTION

The divine avalanche is only the visible beginning of a far greater movement. In God's design, blessing is always in motion.

First it is received.

Then it is transformed.

Then it is directed toward life.

Yet creation also warns us of another possibility. Not all that falls from the mountain nourishes the valleys. Some snow, some water, some provision escapes the life-giving system entirely, rushing beyond its intended course in what mountaineers call the runoff. Though not destroyed, it simply no longer sustains the land from which it came.

Blessing can move this way, too, when it is received without order. When we attempt to trap a blessing, it hardens into stagnation. But when we neglect to guide it, it dissipates, carried away by impulse or unexamined desire. In both cases, what was meant to give life fails to take root.

Stewardship, therefore, is not about how tightly we hold what falls into our hands, but how faithfully we participate in its purpose. We are not just recipients of provision. We are participants in its movement, entrusted to shape and channel what originates in God.

This is how blessing fulfills its design.

It flows through us.

It feeds lives we will never see.

It reaches generations who will never know our names.

The Divine Avalanche as a Cycle
God
Source of All Provision
[I. SETTING THE CONDITIONS]
Pre-Snow and Temperature Drop Phases
[II. THE SNOWFIELDS]
Accumulation of Formation
[III. THE AVALANCHE]
Sudden Release
[IV. THE MELTWATER]
Transformation of Blessing
[V. THE RIVERS]
Flow to Others
[VI. THE VALLEY]
Generational and Communal Nourishment

The Case Study of
JOHNNY BELOVED

Johnny Beloved was thirty years old the day the wire transfer cleared. It was a Tuesday. The number on the screen did not look real. It looked like a typo—too many digits, too much quiet power sitting in a checking account that, just weeks before, had hovered around four figures. His father had been a disciplined man. He was quiet, exact. He was a builder of things no one saw, like real estate deals negotiated in modest offices and partnerships sealed with handshakes and long patience. These were compounding decisions made over decades.

Johnny had never paid attention. He assumed there would always be time.

Now there is only the number: $*7,482,613.21* after taxes. He stares at it the way a child stares at a big wave… unsure whether to run toward it or away from it.

By Thursday, the phone has begun ringing.

"Johnny, buddy, we should talk."

"I've got an opportunity you don't want to miss."

"You're in a position now to make a real impact."

"It would mean a lot if you believed in this."

His college roommate has a startup.

His cousin has a restaurant concept.

A parish acquaintance has a nonprofit expansion.

A crypto consultant sends a pitch deck before Johnny has even responded to the text.

Everyone uses the same tone—

"You're lucky. Now share the luck."

Johnny feels two competing forces: grief for his father, and a rising heat of urgency.

The avalanche has fallen.

Johnny Beloved is not unusual. He is simply early in his formation. Every inheritance, every liquidity event, every business exit, every unexpected bonus, every sudden promotion carries the same question: Is the heart prepared for what the hand now holds?

Now that we have met Johnny and his shocking circumstance, we will walk with him through two possible futures.

In one, Johnny remains unformed.

In the other, he cooperates with grace and is formed by the living God.

One honest admission before we begin. In real life, both Johnnys would have full arcs, with real flaws and real growth. Here they do not. For the sake of time and clarity, I have written each in the extreme—the unformed Johnny at times too careless to be real, the formed Johnny at times closer to a saint than most of us will feel. I have done this on purpose, so the contrast between the ideal and its opposite stays clear. Read them not as finished people, but as two directions a life can take.

Under each letter of AIPOM—Access, Identity, Preparation, Opportunity, and Multiplication—we will observe how formation shapes his decisions, his relationships, the way he stewards what he has been given, and the legacy that follows him.

This is not theory. It is a case study in capacity. Abundance does more than reveal what you have. It reveals who you are. And who you are will determine whether wealth multiplies steadily over decades—or fractures under the weight of urgency, ego, and the FOMO (fear of missing out) that drives both.

Let us begin.

STAGE I

Access

The Pre-Snow Phase

Am I Allowed on the Mountain at All?

BEFORE blessing flows, a door must open. Many people live as though access is restricted, assuming that opportunity and belonging are reserved for others. This posture rarely arises from rebellion. More often, it is shaped by fear, history, exclusion, disappointment, or the subtle conviction that we stand somehow outside the field of grace. When access feels denied, life becomes a landscape of closed doors and guarded rooms that spell out unspoken judgments about who belongs and who does not.

In the language of the mountain, this is the moment before the snow ever falls. The sky is still, the ground is bare. Nothing has yet begun to accumulate. This is the pre-snow phase, the place of positioning.

Here, the question is not about growth or multiplication. It is far more fundamental: "Am I even allowed to be here?" Access answers that question. It is the invitation onto the mountain itself—the assurance that we are not standing outside the story but have been brought into it. Before anything can be released, we must first take our place on the mountain.

> *"He came and proclaimed peace to you who were far off and peace to those who were near; for through him both of us have access in one Spirit to the Father."*
> EPHESIANS 2:17–18

In *Confessions* (X.27.38), St. Augustine of Hippo, who famously struggled with his own carnal desires, gives voice to this interior tension; in modern language it might sound like this: "Too late I loved you. Too late. Beauty so ancient and yet so new. You were already within me, but I was looking everywhere else.... You were with me, but I was not with you." Scholars believe he is not describing divine absence but human disorientation—the experience of searching outward for what was never truly distant. The tragedy is rarely divine distance but human misperception. Access may already exist, yet the human interpretive system can obscure recognition, convincing us that doors are locked which were never closed.

Modern behavioral research confirms what the spiritual tradition has long understood: access shapes perception. When individuals believe they belong in a space, their attention shifts from survival to participation. Behavioral economists Sendhil Mullainathan and Eldar Shafir, in their book *Scarcity: Why Having Too Little Means So Much,* describe how scarcity narrows cognitive bandwidth, making it difficult to perceive opportunity even when it exists. When people operate under scarcity of money, time, social connection, food, or other resources, their attention narrows or "tunnels" toward immediate survival concerns. This tunneling effect can crowd out long-term thinking, limiting the ability to recognize broader possibilities or more strategic solutions.

Scripture announces something radically different. In Christ, access is neither earned through performance nor secured through striving. It is granted through covenant, a covenant sealed in sacrifice and ratified in prayer. The door is not locked; the invitation has already been extended. This section explores what blocks access, how denial cultivates scarcity thinking, and what changes when we recognize that God has already opened the way.

2

Access Granted

When God called Israel his chosen people, he gave them more than land or laws. He gave them access through covenant. Their identity was not built on wealth or armies. It was built on relationship with the creator of heaven and earth. Through that covenant, they were promised his protection and provision, and an inheritance no empire could match.

This understanding of covenant access did not end with Israel, nor did it disappear with the closing pages of Scripture. From the earliest centuries of Christianity, the Church has reflected deeply on what it means to be welcomed into the Father's household through Christ. The early Church Fathers spoke of salvation as adoption into God's family; the saints described prayer as entering the Father's presence; and the popes and the Catechism continue to teach that through Christ we receive access to the Father and share in his inheritance. Across centuries of reflection, the Church has consistently affirmed the same truth: covenant does not merely change our circumstances. It changes our standing before God. Through Christ, the door to the Father is opened.

Long before the Church reflected on these truths, Israel first heard them spoken within the covenant itself.

> *"The Lord will open for you his rich storehouse, the heavens, to give the rain of your land in its season and to bless all your undertakings. You will lend to many nations, but you will not borrow."*
> DEUTERONOMY 28:12

This promise meant Israel was not called to live in dependency but in overflow—to be the head, not the tail, drawing from God's abundance rather than living in fear of scarcity. It was never a guarantee of effortless wealth. It was an invitation into ordered living under God's covenant. The blessing of the storehouse followed obedience and trust, the slow work of formation—never manipulation or entitlement. To "lend and not borrow" was not a symbol of superiority; it was a sign of stability. It described a people formed enough to support others without collapsing themselves, resourced so that generosity did not create dependency or chaos.

CLARIFYING LENDING AND BORROWING

When Scripture speaks of God's people lending and not borrowing, it describes a vision of stability, not a blanket prohibition. In ancient Israel, borrowing was permitted, but it was carefully governed and limited by mercy. Loans among God's people were not to carry interest (Exodus 22:25). Debts were released every seven years under the Sabbatical Year (Deuteronomy 15:1–2). And the Year of Jubilee every fifty years ensured that land was returned to its original families, and indentured servants were set free (Leviticus 25). But when lending to foreigners, interest was permitted and debts could be collected. The law recognized two different kinds of economic relationships—one shaped by covenant mercy, the other by ordinary exchange. Exploitation was a separate concern, addressed elsewhere in the Torah. Outside the covenant, debt followed normal economic rules. Within God's people, debt was restrained so that it would never become permanent bondage.

In other words,

Borrowing was allowed, but exploitation was not.

The Sabbatical Year released debt; Jubilee restored dignity. This distinction matters. The biblical warning is about the weight debt carries. "The borrower is the slave of the lender" (Proverbs 22:7) describes what debt does to a person. It limits freedom and weighs on the soul.

Compare this with modern consumer-lending systems. Today, many people live in economic structures where borrowing is not optional, but structural. In Scripture, debt was temporary and protected. God's economy included mercy cycles. But modern systems often remove those safeguards, allowing debt to become prolonged and compounded. Education, housing, and even emergencies often require resources long before income can catch up. At the same time, many financial decisions are shaped under pressure—driven by fear, urgency, or the promise of security—making people vulnerable to high-interest traps and the illusion of quick money solutions. Borrowing today does not place someone outside of God's will, but it does increase the need for discernment. That is why formation matters so deeply.

We may live in systems that normalize debt, but as heirs of the promise, we are called to respond differently: to stabilize the heart, clarify the reality, order the life, discern the path, and move with peace where possible. And above all, wisdom teaches us that *we must not move faster than our formation.*

COVENANT ACCESS: MORE LESSONS FROM ISRAEL

History also shows that covenant identity formed resilience even in exile and persecution. When foreign empires conquered Israel and many were forced to live outside their homeland, the Israelites preserved their identity through practices that sustained covenant life: Sabbath observance, circumcision, fasting, prayer, and the celebration of holy days. Literacy, strong family structures, and trade networks further sustained Jewish communities across generations. In this context, literacy primarily meant Torah study—the ability to read, recite, and interpret Genesis through Deuteronomy. After the Babylonian exile, Jewish communities gathered regularly to read and explain the Torah, a practice that became foundational to synagogue life. This tradition is vividly illustrated when Nehemiah, the Jewish governor serving under Persian rule, oversaw the rebuilding of Jerusalem's walls and the rededication of the city. As the people gathered, Scripture records:

> *"So they read from the book, from the law of God, with interpretation. They gave the sense, so that the people understood the reading."*
> NEHEMIAH 8:8

Where access was denied in one sphere, God cultivated it in another. Over generations, this covenant-rooted resilience positioned them to steward knowledge, resources, and wisdom in ways that blessed future generations and the broader communities around them. This point matters, because Jewish communities not only sustained covenant identity for future generations but also extended the fruits of that formation to the nations among whom they lived. In the language of the avalanche, wherever they lived—whether in their homeland or in foreign lands—they remained grounded on the mountain of covenant. There they gathered snow steadily through faithfulness and discipline, and in time released an avalanche of blessing that flowed both to their future heirs and to the communities around them.

The lesson is this: poverty is not just the absence of money or resources. It is the absence of covenant access and the practices that grow from it. A poverty mindset keeps a person uninformed, unprepared, and cut off from the resources that create wealth in the first place.

We have all heard the phrase "knowledge is power"—an all-too-familiar refrain. And yet, when we stop seeking knowledge, we slowly close ourselves off from the power that could have shaped us. Poverty denies us access to circles where wealth-building conversations are happening. It keeps us out of the rooms where deals get made over dinner and opportunities change hands in hallways.

Wealthy people do not simply "have money"; they think differently about opportunity.

Affluent people look for patterns and access points. They also search for environments where possibility grows. They position themselves near information, mentors, and communities that cultivate wisdom.

Picture this: if you never spend time near mountains, you never think about avalanches. I live in Florida. An avalanche is the farthest thing from my mind. Over here, we have hurricanes, sinkholes, undertows, thunderstorms, floods, swamps, and extreme heat to keep us occupied. But I imagine that if my family intentionally positioned itself near a mountain where snow is steadily building, our mindset would change. We would start to anticipate what could happen.

Avalanches require three ingredients:

1) A mountain (the setting)
2) Heavy accumulation of snow (the weather pattern)
3) Gravity (the force)

Remove any one of those, and an avalanche cannot happen. Wealth works the same way:

The setting is the *environment* where wealthy people operate—the networks, the rooms, the industries. If you never put yourself in the right setting, you will never have to worry about an avalanche, but you will also never experience the avalanche of opportunity and blessing that wealth can bring. (And of course, like me, you may still have to worry about the alligators and mosquitoes in your part of the world.)

The weather pattern is the *steady build-up* of knowledge, habits, and disciplines that pile up like snow, as well as the weak layers built into the dry slab.

The gravitational force is the *sustaining power* that never rests. Gravity is that constant downward pull God built into creation that is always there, always reliable, acting on whatever lies in its path. Without the gravity that holds our atmosphere in place, life as we know it could not exist. The snow does not generate gravity by moving; the snow moves *because* of it, once conditions are right. In our lives, it represents the sustaining power of God, who upholds the created order at every moment and acts within it. Our part is not to generate that force but to cooperate with it.

Faith is obedience meeting the force God supplies.

Scripture shows us repeatedly that God's power meets human obedience at the moment of trust. Some of the clearest examples come from Israel's entry into the Promised Land. Rahab welcomed the spies before deliverance was visible (Joshua 2:1–7). The priests stepped into the Jordan while the waters were still flowing, and only then did the river part (Joshua 3:9–17). Israel marched around Jericho for seven days before a single wall fell (Joshua 6:2–20). In every case, the promise existed, but movement agreed with it. As Scripture reminds us:

> *"Faith by itself, if it has no works, is dead."*
> JAMES 2:17

Now some of you might say, "Here we go again. If we talk about access without mentioning real structural barriers that have existed in America, then this book just doesn't see my reality. End of story." You are right that sometimes poverty has been the result of discriminatory lending practices, segregated neighborhoods, limited educational opportunities, and exclusion from financial systems that shaped generations. These realities should humble us, not shame us, because they remind us that access is never only personal:

- It is social, because it grows within communities shaped by relationships, networks, and opportunities that are not equally shared.
- It is spiritual, because our hope, identity, and dignity ultimately rest in God and in the covenant we share with Christ, who draws us into his own sonship with the Father.
- And it is structural, because policies and programs can either widen doors of opportunity or keep them closed.

But those structural barriers do not contradict the thesis of this book; they explain why covenant formation *matters even more.* Even in those places of exclusion, covenant identity created resilience.

Where doors were shut, God formed new pathways.

Where systems withheld opportunity, faith communities built their own networks, schools, businesses, and ministries. Covenant does not erase injustice, but it refuses to let injustice have the final word.

That is why formation cannot be separated from identity. Without God, there is no anchor. And if there is no anchor, there is no grounding in our identity. And if there is no identity, there is no inheritance. And if there is no inheritance, there is no overflow of grace, wisdom, provision, and fruit that spills and multiplies beyond our capacity.

Formation teaches an even deeper truth—not every room builds wisdom. Access alone is not enough. The real issue is whether we are standing *in the right room.* In the language of the avalanche, the question is not simply whether we are near the mountain, but whether we are standing on the kind of ground that teaches us how to read the snow, discern the slope, and recognize what can bear weight. Not every place on a mountain is safe or instructive.

But with covenant, even in adversity, there is access to wisdom, provision, and renewal. For us today, in Christ, that covenant expands; it is no longer limited to one people or one land.

Through his cross, the dividing walls fall, and those who were far off are welcomed near.

The promises are no longer written only in stone or guarded by a Temple curtain; they are sealed in his blood and carried in our hearts. In Christ, we are invited into the same relationship of trust and faithfulness that God established with Israel, but opened now to all nations, all stories, all histories. What Israel tasted in part, we inherit in fullness: peace with the Father, access through the Spirit, and a life rooted not in scarcity but in the generosity of God himself.

> *"And my God will fully satisfy every need of yours according to his riches in glory in Christ Jesus."*
> PHILIPPIANS 4:19

> *"The thief comes only to steal and kill and destroy. I came that they may have life, and have it abundantly."*
> JOHN 10:10

Covenant, then, is not a shortcut to wealth or a shield from hardship. It is the identity that anchors us when circumstances shift and systems fail. It roots our lives in a God who provides differently than the world does—sometimes through resources, sometimes through wisdom, sometimes through endurance—but always through the grace secured by the blood Christ poured out at Calvary.

In Christ, access is no longer limited by history, status, or human permission. The door is open. And when God opens access, he invites us to move forward with intention, to let him shape our hearts and to steward what he places in our hands so that the blessing does not end with us but rather flows through us to others.

THE COVENANT AND GRANDMOTHER'S HOUSE

Now consider how everything connects within God's divine avalanche:

1) The mountain represents our *covenant space* where we can safely have a covenant relationship with God, a "Mount of Belonging" established through the redeeming work of Christ. No lineage or striving can earn it. God changed all that. Now covenant is a relationship grace gives, handed down from God.

Think of your grandmother's house. It was never special because of the square footage or the furniture. It was not even the smell of the kitchen, though that certainly helped. It was the relationship you had with her *inside the house*—the knowledge that you were expected, that your place at the table was already set, that belonging there required nothing from you but your presence. That is covenant. Through the blood of Christ, a new ground of belonging is established—not earned, not inherited through family name, but given. Without that grounding, blessing can arrive and still feel unstable, like being a guest in a house where you are not sure you are welcome. With it, the foundation settles because you finally know whose house you are in.

> *"For this reason he is the mediator of a new covenant, so that those who are called may receive the promised eternal inheritance…."*
> HEBREWS 9:15

Jesus himself speaks this reality plainly:

> *"...This cup that is poured out for you is the new covenant in my blood."*
> LUKE 22:20

And the Apostle Paul reminds us:

> *"But now in Christ Jesus you who once were far off have been brought near by the blood of Christ."*
> EPHESIANS 2:13

2) The snow represents the *steady accumulation of wisdom*. Like snow gathering layer upon layer, formation builds gradually over time.

In grandmother's house, the snow would be everything that accumulated *inside* the relationship over time—the Sunday dinners you never missed, the phone calls you made just to check in, the times you showed up when it was inconvenient, the lessons she taught you that you did not fully understand until years later. None of it felt significant in the moment. But layer by layer, it formed you into someone who knew how to receive what she had to give. Think of everything that built up inside your grandmother's house over the years (not the cookies, but the formation). The way she handled a fixed income without panic. The way she prayed before meals without making a production out of it. The way she gave without keeping score. You absorbed all those things without knowing you were being shaped by them. Layer by layer, those moments settled into something load-bearing.

Each act of trust and each choice aligned with covenant adds to the layers—not always visible, but deeply consequential when the season turns. Even systems that seem sudden are built this way. Take the lottery: what looks like an instant windfall rests on years of careful planning, regulation, and accountability designed to earn public trust. By the time someone buys a ticket, a long process of formation has already taken place beneath the surface.

3) The gravity represents *the constant sustaining power of God,* always present and always reliable. The avalanche releases not because that power switches on, but because the prepared ground has finally reached the season when what God supplies can move.

On prepared ground, its blessings may take many forms: an unexpected peace that quiets long-held anxiety, the restoration of strained or broken relationships, clarity after seasons of confusion, provision where lack once dominated, healed finances, renewed purpose, resilience in hardship, open doors, protection from unseen dangers, or favor beyond calculation. Such an avalanche may reshape many dimensions of life: relational, material, vocational, circumstantial, protective, directional, and yes, even financial.

In grandmother's house, gravity is what happens when all that formation finally has somewhere to go. You are standing in your own kitchen, and without thinking, you have made enough for whoever might stop by. Or you sit with a friend in crisis and find that you have created a safe space with words and presence, and you realize you learned that posture at your grandmother's table without ever being taught it directly. Formation always flows *outward and downward*—toward others, toward the valley, toward those who need what the mountain has gathered. You spent years receiving at her house, absorbing without knowing you were being shaped. Then one day you find yourself doing what she did, showing up for someone else, giving without judgment, handling difficulty without panic. The power just moved through you. That is gravity doing its sustaining work. That is formation meeting it and reaching its season.

To stand within covenant is to recognize that the release of blessing is not driven by human effort alone, but by divine timing. Israel's history reveals this pattern repeatedly. When covenant identity and lived trust aligned, seasons of remarkable provision and lasting protection often followed. Scripture records moments when communities rooted in covenant found peace in the midst of turmoil and abundance where scarcity should have ruled. Wisdom came to them when everyone around them was grasping for it. These blessings were never merely material. They included families that held together across generations, leaders wise enough to guide their people, sacred knowledge passed safely on, and a people whose identity stayed anchored in God when others drifted.

In Christ, this inheritance is not erased. It is widened. What began within Israel's covenantal life is now extended to all nations through the new covenant established by Jesus. Covenant access therefore speaks of more than coins or possessions. It points to a deeper inheritance: disciplined hearts, wisdom that keeps growing, peace within, relationships restored, endurance through hardship, and favor that often appears in quiet and unexpected ways. These are the fruits of a life rooted in belonging to God.

Access is not just a nice intellectual idea. You know you have been to your grandmother's house when you've shared a meal around her table. The photo albums lie open on the coffee table. The toys and board games are worn through. The completed puzzle still occupies the dining room table. Empty lemonade glasses sit in the sink. Your skin still smells of chlorine from hours in the pool. The cookie jar is nearly empty. You've been hugged goodbye, and your soul comes home rested. The story of covenant, therefore, points beyond material provision toward something greater: a people formed by trust and obedience, sustained by the presence of the living God.

God Is Not the Mountain

Some readers may instinctively assume that the mountain represents God himself. Scripture frequently places mountains at moments of divine encounter. Moses ascends Sinai. Zion is where God plants his name and dwells among his people. The Mount of Transfiguration is the moment Christ's divine nature is unveiled to Peter, James, and John.

But covenant is not "being on top of God." Mountains belong to creation. God is the uncreated source of all creation. Mountains often function symbolically, suggesting strength, permanence, and transcendence—the kind of perspective that comes from standing above the landscape, qualities readily associated with God. Yet God is not an element within the landscape; he is its author. He is not the mountain itself but the *telos* toward which all covenant life moves—the summit that gives meaning to ascent rather than the terrain upon which it occurs.

In Scripture, mountains most often signify placement, where one is standing and established. Covenant, however, is relationship with God, not just proximity to him. In avalanche theology, the mountain represents the stable ground of belonging secured through covenant. In your grandmother's house, it is literally the house itself, which functions as a domestic covenant space. It is where belonging is established, where identity is formed, where the faithful practices of a well-lived life are absorbed without being taught.

The mountain also offers something else: strategic protection. In times of war, high ground was not a luxury but a necessity. It gave the watchman sight lines over the surrounding terrain, early warning against approaching threats, and a natural defense against invasion, tribal conflict, and predatory danger. Flood waters rise from below. The mountain stands firm above them.

Your grandmother's house operates the same way. It is elevated ground in the truest sense—a place where the soul has sight lines, where danger is seen before it arrives, where the child is held above the chaos of the surrounding world. You were safe there not because nothing difficult existed, but because you were positioned above it, held within something solid enough to withstand it. In this way, your grandmother and God operate by the same logic. Both the house and the mountain are where the covenant relationship resides safely away from danger. (Please note: not every mountain is stable, and not every house is safe. If that is your story, this book does not look away from it. The good news is that God does not require a perfect inheritance to begin a faithful one. He has been known to start entirely new lines from broken ground, as we will see later with the story of Abraham and the first divine avalanche.)

For now, hold this truth:

To stand firm on the mountain is to stand firm in covenant identity.

PHYSICAL LAWS VS. DIVINE INITIATION

In avalanche science, gravity is the constant force acting upon the snowpack; the load finally moves when conditions reach their tipping point. Avalanches result from the interaction of snowpack structure, slope angle, shifting temperatures, and external triggers—all natural occurrences that work autonomously within the laws of physics. Divine sovereignty upholds created processes rather than competing with them, establishing the conditions under which movement—spiritual or material—becomes possible in its proper season. God ordinarily governs the world through the faithful order of creation, yet at times he acts with particular redemptive purpose. However, the existence of a natural process should not be confused with a specific divine commission. While all avalanches operate within the physical laws God has authored, not every avalanche can be attributed to direct divine initiation. What can be stated with confidence, however, is that every avalanche, whether natural or metaphorical, reveals the integrity or instability of the ground beneath it.

CLOSING REFLECTION

God invites us to move from denial—the posture that assumes the door is locked—into access. From there, we step into the provision he is already making available. For many people, however, denial did not begin as unbelief. It was learned through history. Experiences of exclusion, discrimination, loss, or systemic barriers have taught entire communities to assume that certain doors were never meant to open for them. Such histories humble us and remind us that access has not always been experienced evenly, and that scarcity thinking is often a response of survival rather than a failure of faith.

Yet it is precisely here that covenant identity becomes most meaningful. When access has been denied by human systems, God does not withdraw; *he draws nearer.* Many still live as though the door remains locked, not because God has locked it, but because history taught them to expect refusal. In this posture, opportunity feels withheld and abundance appears reserved for others.

Covenant announces a deeper truth: access is not ultimately determined by social permission or past exclusion, but by God's initiative. What history restricted, covenant restores. Fear taught us to stand outside, but God now invites us in with heads lifted, trusting freely. Scripture tells this story with unmistakable clarity. It bears repeating:

> *"[T]hrough him both of us have access in one Spirit to the Father."*
> EPHESIANS 2:18

Perhaps you already know what this feels like. Maybe there was a grandmother, or someone who played that role—a kitchen that always had enough, a table where you were expected, a porch light that was always on when you arrived, and a presence that asked nothing of you but your arrival. You did not earn your place there; you were simply known. That is the texture of covenant access. God's household runs on the same logic, only deeper and without limit.

Access is not earned through striving; it is granted through covenant and deepened through formation.

The door was not locked… it was never locked. What kept us outside was not his refusal but our own learned expectation of rejection—the long habit of assuming we did not belong. Covenant says otherwise. And formation is how we learn to believe it.

Covenant was never a promise of ease.

It is a promise of belonging.

Standing on the mountain has never been about controlling the avalanche. It is about trusting the one who sends the snow and governs the seasons. In Christ, access is received as a gift. It cannot be bought, earned, or even inherited. Every generation stands before the same open door on the same terms.

Access exists. The real question is whether we are willing to live as people who believe it. Our task, then, is to remain rooted, allowing faith to deepen with time. Wisdom accumulates of its own accord. Obedience settles like snow upon the soul. And beneath it all, the sustaining power of God never rests—always present, always reliable. We do not generate the force; we lean into it with faith. In due season, the divine avalanche releases and the prepared heart sees it for what it is: grace in motion.

Johnny Beloved and Access

Access is the first avalanche layer. If Johnny misinterprets access, every letter that follows—Identity, Preparation, Opportunity, Multiplication—will tilt toward instability. But if access is understood as covenant, the snow begins to settle correctly. Access is not about entering every room. It is about standing firmly in the right one. The difference between access and formation becomes clearer when we watch how two versions of the same person respond to sudden wealth.

UNFORMED JOHNNY

The money clears.
He leaves it there.
He stares at it daily.
He screenshots it.
He feels powerful.
He starts wiring from it impulsively.

By Friday, Johnny has three dinners scheduled. The invitations come fast: steakhouse, private club, rooftop lounge. Rooms he has never entered before now open without resistance. He notices how quickly people return his calls, how quickly his presence becomes valuable.

For the first time in his life, Johnny feels included.

Access feels like arrival. He mistakes invitation for belonging. His friend's attorney introduces him to "a few people you should know." Within weeks, Johnny is sitting at tables where capital moves quickly:

- ❄ Venture funds
- ❄ Hedge funds
- ❄ Real estate syndications
- ❄ High-yield opportunities presented with casual confidence

Johnny nods often. He does not ask many questions. He assumes access means qualification. He assumes proximity means readiness. When his college roommate pitches a tech platform, Johnny writes a $250,000 check before fully understanding the burn rate. When a parish acquaintance mentions a "kingdom expansion opportunity," Johnny pledges six figures without reviewing financial statements. He believes generosity requires speed. He believes delay signals fear.

What he does not understand is this: Access without formation amplifies insecurity.

Johnny's social media becomes his mountain. Notifications slide into his DMs like snow. He feels important, but he is afraid to say no. He fears exclusion more than he fears misallocation. He mistakes popularity for access and affirmation for identity. He does not realize that covenant access means relationship with God—not room entry. He does not see that he has entered rooms where the avalanche of urgency is already unstable. Within months, Johnny's calendar is full. His capital is fragmented. And though he has more access than ever, he has less clarity than before.

Formed Johnny

The money clears.

Johnny closes the laptop.

He lets it sit.

His father's advisors will eventually remind him that idle capital carries its own risks, but that conversation can wait.

He does not call anyone.

Formation looks different in every life. For some it is a grandmother's kitchen. For Johnny, it is his father's study. He walks to the small wooden desk and opens the worn leather Bible still resting there. He remembers something his father once said over coffee: "Access is a responsibility, son. Not a spotlight."

Johnny does not rush into rooms. He asks first: "Why has this been entrusted to me?"

When invitations come, he listens, but slowly.

He does not equate access with obligation. He understands covenant. Access is not proof of superiority. It is proximity to stewardship.

When a venture capitalist invites him to a private investor circle, Johnny responds: "I'd like to observe for a season before committing capital." When his roommate pitches his startup, Johnny asks questions—then goes home and learns. He researches ideas he has never needed before:

- Audited projections
- Corporate structure
- Timeline clarity

These are things only access could have made him curious about. Proximity has awakened an appetite he did not know he had. That appetite serves him when a parish acquaintance proposes expansion. Johnny asks questions and listens carefully, measuring the answers against what he has been quietly studying. He is not yet an expert, but he is no longer reactive. He understands that Israel's covenant access was never license for recklessness. It is stability. To lend and not borrow requires strength beneath the surface.

Johnny positions himself intentionally:

- He leaves messages with his father's three closest advisors: his tax accountant, his certified financial planner, and his estate planning attorney.
- He curates his closest confidants, choosing proximity to people already formed in what he is still learning.
- He joins a small circle of disciplined investors rather than the loudest rooms.

Johnny recognizes that proximity shapes mindset. Just as living near mountains teaches you to read snow conditions, living near disciplined capital teaches you to read access. He understands that poverty is not merely lack of money or a scarcity mindset; it is lack of intentional exposure to wisdom. So he places himself in environments of formation before stepping into deployment. He does not rush to "be in the room." He chooses which mountain to stand on—the mountain of covenant, where God grants true perspective over the surrounding terrain—and refuses to let public opinion or ambition be that mountain. And because he stands on covenant identity rather than social approval, access does not inflate him. It anchors him.

STAGE II

Identity

The Temperature Drop Phase

Who Am I Now That I Am Here?

ACCESS answers where we can go. Identity, however, answers who we are when we arrive. Before God entrusts inheritance, he establishes belonging.

In grandmother's house, access got you through the door. But identity is what allowed you to sit down without apology—to eat her food, to kick off your shoes, to sink into her couch, to receive those sentimental birthday cards without needing to count what was inside.

Throughout Scripture, identity always precedes assignment. God names his people before he leads them. He calls them his own before any gift or task is laid upon them. This section explores covenant identity: sonship received, not achieved. It also examines how poverty thinking often survives even after access is granted, and how unsettled identity can turn blessing into a burden.

In avalanche science, temperature determines whether snow melts away or remains long enough to accumulate. In the same way, identity determines whether blessing simply passes through us or whether it can settle within us. A heart that does not know who it is cannot safely carry what it receives. Furthermore, standing on the mountain means learning to live from who God says we are, rather than from fear or the need to measure up. Identity anchors the soul to the mountain of covenant. Without it, access becomes unstable and blessing becomes anxiety. With it, the heart steadies and stewardship matures. From there, everything else flows.

> *"If children, then heirs, heirs of God and joint heirs with Christ…."*
> ROMANS 8:17

3

Identity Changes Everything

Standing on the mountain means learning to live from who God says we are when we leave grandmother's house and enter the rooms of life. Access can place you in the room, but identity tells you whether you belong there. In other words, access changes posture but identity changes everything.

Identity is not learned only through doctrine; it is often discovered through the quiet work God does in our own story. I once knew a woman whose life crossed mine along many of the same paths. We were both new mothers in the local chapter of the Moms Club, and later, we became band parents and swim parents, entering the same rooms and standing on the same sidelines. Yet our inner posture could not have been more different. When I walked into a space for the first time, my unspoken question was:

"Do I belong here?"

When she entered, her presence seemed to declare:

"How can I serve now that I am here?"

We had the same access, the same invitations, the same roles. But she carried a quiet confidence that never seemed to question her right to be there. Her identity felt settled; her presence, assured. I, on the other hand, was still wrestling with my own sense of belonging. As the new mother of three boys, I often felt like an imposter, uncertain whether I was measuring up, uncertain whether I truly fit. While other mothers appeared to step naturally into their identity, I lingered on the threshold, trying to convince myself that I had a place in the room at all.

Access can give you proximity to opportunity, but…

Identity gives you the confidence to receive access, steward it, and remain when the doors close behind you.

Without identity, access produces anxiety, comparison, and the fear of being exposed. With identity, access produces peace, courage, and the freedom to act without striving. Before God entrusts responsibility, he establishes belonging.

While Scripture has always known this truth, modern psychology arrives at a similar conclusion. Developmental psychologist Erik Erikson, in *Identity: Youth and Crisis*, describes identity formation as a central task of human development, one that must be sufficiently established before individuals can commit to roles, relationships, and vocation. When identity has yet to be settled, individuals often experience what Erikson termed "role confusion," marked by uncertainty about belonging, difficulty with commitment, and heightened sensitivity to social approval. In this state, even opportunity can feel threatening rather than empowering.

Here is the bottom line: social access can be granted, revoked, or earned. But identity, once received in Christ, is *secured.* Your identity does not rise and fall with markets, approval, or circumstance. When your life is rooted in covenant identity rather than social permission, you no longer ask, "Do I deserve to be here?" Rather, you ask, "How am I called to serve here?" That shift transforms not only how you enter rooms, but how you walk through life itself. Once we realize the door is not locked, the next question becomes… who are we when we walk through it?

Before God releases provision, he anchors identity.

We prepare for abundance not by grasping for more, but by standing firmly in who we are before him. You cannot claim what you do not believe belongs to you. Psychiatrist John Bowlby, in his seminal work *Attachment*, demonstrated that children explore the world most confidently when they are securely connected to a trusted caregiver. Secure attachment fosters confidence and curiosity, while insecurity often leads to anxiety and hesitation. In the language of attachment, God may come to be experienced as an internalized secure presence—a constant source of safety, belonging, and rest for the human heart. This is not merely poetic language; it is increasingly reflected in psychological research on attachment to God, religious coping, and spiritual models of attachment. Healing, then, often unfolds through a convergence of means:

1) The presence of trustworthy relationships that offer consistency and care.
2) The quiet work of interior reflection and growth.
3) A deepening spiritual identity rooted in belonging rather than striving.

Over time, the nervous system begins to settle, expectations of abandonment gradually loosen, and identity becomes more stable and grounded. This is not accidental. God designed the human body to require rest. He *built the Sabbath* into the rhythm of creation not as a suggestion but as a reflection of how we are made—creatures who need to stop, to be still, to remember that we are held. Jesus Himself restored this vision when he declared, "The sabbath was made for humankind, and not humankind for the sabbath" (Mark 2:27). Sabbath is not a burden imposed upon God's children; it is a gift given to us. It teaches us, week after week, that our value is rooted not in what we produce but in whose we are. A nervous system at rest—not just physically but also mentally—is not a passive or weak thing; it is a system operating as God intended.

The modern world runs on a different logic entirely. Algorithms are engineered to exploit restlessness, cycling through clickbait, manufactured urgency, curated desire, and ambient fear. Covenant identity was never designed to run on that frantic, hectic frequency. In fact, the high-octane pace leads to a level of burnout that separates us from our very foundation.

A settled person, however, is harder to manipulate.

Scripture reveals that spiritual confidence grows from knowing we belong to the Father. God, it seems, consistently establishes identity before inheritance. The Israelites did not enter the Promised Land until they first received covenant identity at the mountain. Before they moved forward, they were named, formed, and bound to God as his people. The mountain was not merely geography; it was the place of belonging.

Our mountain is different, yet the pattern remains. For those in Christ, identity is not rooted in effort, performance, or circumstance, but in sonship—a received identity, not an achieved one. This is a profoundly Pauline vision of the spiritual life: that identity is received through adoption and grace; that worth is not earned through performance; and that obedience flows from belonging rather than striving toward it. To live from sonship is to live from the awareness of being a child and heir of God rather than a performer seeking approval. The Apostle Paul expresses this with striking clarity:

> *"For all who are led by the Spirit of God are children of God. For you did not receive a spirit of slavery to fall back into fear, but you have received a spirit of adoption. When we cry, 'Abba! Father!' it is that very Spirit bearing witness with our spirit that we are children of God, and if children, then heirs, heirs of God and joint heirs with Christ...."*
>
> ROMANS 8:14–17

When our sense of self is secured in this belonging, the pull of the endless scroll begins to lose its grip. We are no longer searching for something to confirm our worth or calm our anxiety. We already know whose we are.

Sabbath, in this sense, is not merely a practice. It is a declaration of identity as joint heirs with Christ, the act of a people who trust that the world will not fall apart if they stop performing. What was once fractured is not erased, but gently reordered… redeemed and re-patterned into something capable of receiving and sustaining love.

Access flows from this truth: what we receive in life is deeply shaped by what we believe about who we are. When identity is unsettled, abundance can feel foreign, something we're not sure we deserve and are almost afraid to trust. A poverty mindset clings to names like *poor, unlucky, forgotten, unwanted.* A covenant mindset rests in what God has already spoken: *chosen, adopted, equipped, heir, beloved… wanted.* Yes, wanted. For years I struggled to believe that God truly wanted me, and that his heart toward me was good. I would read…

> *"If you then, who are evil, know how to give good gifts to your children, how much more will your Father in heaven give good things to those who ask him!"*
> MATTHEW 7:11

…and I heard the promise, but it did not quite find a home in me.

St. Thérèse of Lisieux—a young Carmelite nun whose "little way" of childlike trust in God's mercy revealed a profound path to holiness—came to understand that God's love is not reserved for the great or the accomplished but is poured out freely upon those who approach him in their littleness. "He willed to create great souls comparable to lilies and roses, but He has created smaller ones and these must be content to be daisies or violets destined to give joy to God's glances when He looks down at His feet" (*Story of a Soul*, Manuscript A). Like St. Thérèse, I struggled to believe that such love could be meant for someone as ordinary as me. As the child of exiles shaped by loss and survival, love often meant safety, opportunity, and rebuilding what had been taken. After displacement under Castro's regime, freedom and material stability became symbols of protection, and, in many ways, of love itself. Without realizing it, I learned to measure goodness by what could be secured.

Part of my struggle with identity also grew out of my relationship with my mother. As the child of immigrants learning to find their place in a new country, I was already navigating questions of belonging. By nature, I was a gentle child—I would give my lunch to the hungry student, surrender my turn on the swing to the sad child, and sometimes even hold back my athletic abilities so that teammates would feel more confident. But at home, shaped by the experience of being foreigners in an unfamiliar land, kindness was often viewed as a liability. My mother feared that too gentle a nature might leave me vulnerable in a difficult world, and in her own wounded way she tried to harden me against it. Those early lessons left me unsure whether the kindness God placed in me was a strength or a weakness, and that uncertainty followed me into many of the rooms I later entered.

It was in this interior confusion that God began to meet me. In the quiet of the Adoration Chapel, he has been gently untangling that story—not erasing my history, because I remain deeply proud of our family's survival, but re-anchoring it. He is teaching me that my truest identity is not found in heritage, nation, or even strength of character, but in belonging to him: a child of the one who created the heavens, the earth, and the entire cosmos, ordered and sustained by his hand.

His desire for us runs deeper than survival, and his goodness is not fragile or scarce.

Slowly, God is persuading my heart, not with arguments but through his manifest presence, that I am wanted and that his intentions toward me are kind. And in that kindness, I am beginning to see something I once doubted: that the gentleness God placed within me is not a weakness to be overcome, *but a strength that reflects his own heart.* When kindness is mistaken for weakness, it often reveals not a flaw in the one who offers the kindness and gentleness, but a misunderstanding of the God whose character it reflects. Christ himself taught us to "turn the other cheek," not as an invitation to accept abuse, but as a declaration that our dignity does not depend on the blows of this world.

A mountain holds its shape regardless of the weather that passes over it.

Neither should we allow rejection, criticism, or suffering to redefine who we are. Identity is formed at the summit, not in the storm. And what others say or do to the mortal body cannot measure against the eternal hope of a soul destined for life with God. Formation, then, is not the hardening of the heart, but rather its alignment with the character of God himself. To be formed in Christ is to become the kind of person whose life effectively reflects the heart of the Father.

In time I began to realize that my encounters in Adoration were not unique to me. The experience of being met by God with love and identity lies at the very heart of the Christian life. As Pope Benedict XVI writes in *Deus Caritas Est* (2005), Christianity begins with encounter, not ideology: "Being Christian is not the result of an ethical choice or a lofty idea, but the encounter with an event, a person, which gives life a new horizon and a decisive direction." And it is this encounter that is transforming me: that everything else in the life of faith flows from the belief that we are held by a powerful but gentle Father who delights to give. I am no longer living out of the old story of scarcity and unworthiness. I am learning to live under a new identity as a child who belongs, and from that belonging everything else begins to flow.

Standing on the mountain means allowing God's declaration to speak louder than every lesser voice.

In the Catholic Church, many hearts carry mother and father wounds, and grace often meets people there through intercession. Some find consolation in asking the Blessed Mother to pray for them, letting her tenderness draw them toward the Father's love, and for others it might be St. Joseph, whose quiet strength and faithful fatherhood offer a healing image of protection and care. Others are helped by the story of a particular saint whose life feels familiar and accessible, like St. Thérèse of Lisieux. This was a revelation to me, especially as I continue to heal my own mother-wound and sort out how I feel about the Holy Family. Yet the Church keeps reminding me of something steady and beautiful: whether comfort comes through a familiar saint or the Holy Family, it is always and only *through Jesus Christ* that our identity is formed. And it is the Holy Spirit—the one beyond our human categories of gender—who bears witness within us that we are children of God. These mediators do not replace the Father; they lead us to him. And in that leading, I am discovering what it means to stand on the mountain, not anchored in ethnicity, biography, or even wounds, but in the steady identity of belonging to a creator who calls me his heiress.

St. Cyprian of Carthage expressed this belonging with striking simplicity: "He can no longer have God for his Father who has not the Church for his mother" (*On the Unity of the Church*, I.6). The Catechism of the Catholic Church echoes this same truth, teaching that "the dignity of man rests above all on the fact that he is called to communion with God" (CCC 27). Pope John Paul II, reflecting on the human condition at the dawn of his pontificate, reminds us of the foundation beneath all identity: "Man cannot live without love" (*Redemptor Hominis*, 10).

Ironically, I recently learned that I may be a direct descendant of early 17th-century English colonist John Rogers, as well as Dutch settler Josias J. De Raet, later known as Josias Driggs. This lineage eventually reached the Caribbean, where in 1832 a descendant named Elias William Driggs, born in the Bahamas, married Rosa Aguilera of Holguín, Cuba. I am also descended from Hezekiah Hubbard, who supported the American Revolution by supplying essential provisions to the Continental Army. That final connection would qualify me for membership in the Daughters of the American Revolution (DAR). As a child of Hispanic immigrants, these ancestral revelations surprised me. After the initial shock wore off, it even amused me, because in one sense it meant my roots in this country reach back further than many people I meet. Yet the discovery also reminded me of something deeper: ancestry, heritage, and national stories may shape us, but they do not define us. My truest identity is not found in any lineage of this world, but in belonging to the Father who calls me his daughter.

When identity is rooted in the love of the Father and secured through our adoption in Christ, we no longer stand on the mountain asking whether we belong—

We stand on the mountain ready to live, serve, and steward what God entrusts to us.

As a swim and band mom, I often felt unsure of my place. But through the avalanche metaphor and through the quiet grace of Adoration, where God gently calls me his own, my identity is being experientially settled. I sense that when I one day become a grandmother, my house will be the place of unconditional love and unlimited formation. The door will always be open. The food will always be warm. And no child who crosses that threshold will ever need to count what is inside the card—because they will already know without being told that they are wanted. And when I leave the house and enter the rooms of life, I will no longer be asking what I am doing there. I will already know the answer: "How can I serve now that I am here?"

CLOSING REFLECTION

Identity is not something we achieve. It is something we receive, often slowly, often uneventfully, as God patiently teaches the heart to believe what has always been true. The question is no longer, "Do I belong?" but "Will I live as though I do?"

Many of us spend years standing at the threshold of rooms God has already opened, waiting for permission that has already been given. The orphan asks, "How do I earn a place?" The son asks, "How do I faithfully steward what has already been entrusted to me?"

The mountain, therefore, is not a place of audition; it is a place of identity. To stand on the mountain is to stand as one who is already known, already loved, already named. From that place of belonging, everything changes. Every Sabbath becomes a rehearsal for eternity. By ceasing from ordinary labor, we proclaim that we are no longer slaves striving to earn a place in the household but sons and daughters who already belong there. Every week becomes a confession that our inheritance is received, not earned.

Practical Application: Establishing Identity

If you are accustomed to speaking daily affirmations into a mirror, this exercise will feel natural. However, if you are more inclined, like me, toward quiet reflection, begin each day by prayerfully proclaiming that you are a beloved son or daughter of the Most High God and a co-heir with Christ. Gently replace the language of lack and exclusion with the language of covenant and belonging, anchored in a Father who is both kind and faithful, whose love for you does not waver.

Identity is not something you manufacture or achieve; it is something God has already spoken, which the heart gradually learns to trust, receive, and live from. As your confidence shifts from your performance to his promises, striving begins to give way to rest.

The Sabbath is not the reward of our identity; it is one of its privileges. Our role is not to invent identity but to agree with grace, receive it with gratitude, and live from what God has already declared to be true.

Reader's Prayer: Declaration of Identity

Father, I stand before You as Your child.
Not by merit, not by performance, not by strength—
but because You have called me, adopted me,
and named me as Your own.
You have placed Your Spirit within me, a kind and gentle spirit,
and the Spirit Himself bears witness that I belong to You.
I am not a stranger. I am not an outsider.
Like a grandmother who loves without condition,
You show me I am welcomed, wanted, and loved.
I renounce every false name that has shaped my story—
poverty, unworthiness, abandonment, fear, scarcity.
I reject the lies of the enemy:
that kindness makes me weak or invites abuse,
that blessing belongs to others and not to me,
and that provision is something I must chase or prove I deserve.
I receive the truth of covenant:
that I am chosen, seen, and held by a faithful Father.
My identity is not fragile.
My inheritance is not uncertain.
My place in Your household is secure.
Teach my heart to rest.
Teach my spirit to trust.
Teach me to recognize Your goodness without fear.
Today, I choose to stand on the mountain—
to live from identity instead of anxiety,
from access instead of denial,
from gratitude instead of fear,
from belonging instead of striving.
Form in me a heart that listens,
a spirit that obeys,

and a mind anchored in Your truth.
May every decision, every opportunity, and every resource
flow from this unshakeable truth:
I am Your child—and if a child, then an heir.
Today I walk forward not as one excluded,
but as one invited into Your purpose,
trusting the access You have already granted
through Jesus Christ, my Lord and Savior.
Amen.

Johnny Beloved and Identity

Johnny has inherited millions. Access placed him in rooms. Identity, however, will determine whether he stands in them or walks away. Johnny's inheritance is the same in both scenarios. The difference is internal architecture. If he believes he must prove he deserves the mountain, he will spend his inheritance trying to defend it. If he believes he is already a son, he will steward the mountain without fear.

UNFORMED JOHNNY

The first time someone introduces him as "Johnny Beloved… his father left him quite a portfolio," Johnny feels a strange tightening in his chest. He does not know whether he is proud or exposed. He begins checking his account balance daily, not because it changes much, but because it steadies him. The number becomes reassurance.

Then comparison begins.

❄ Who else inherited this young?
❄ Who is ahead of me?
❄ What are they doing with their money?

He upgrades his watch. Then he buys a new car. Then he finds a bigger apartment. He does not level up extravagantly—just enough to "match the room." He tells himself he is not showing off. But something subtle is happening: his inheritance is no longer something entrusted. It is something proving worth.

Without noticing, Johnny begins answering the question "Who am I?" with the response "I am the one who has." When markets fluctuate, he feels personal instability. When a deal underperforms, he feels small. When a friend lands a bigger exit, he feels threatened.

Access gives him proximity. Unsettled identity turns proximity into performance. He says yes to opportunities he does not fully believe in—not because they align, but because he fears irrelevance.

The Sabbath feels impractical to him. One day without networking, monitoring markets, or pursuing the next opportunity seems irresponsible. Rest feels like falling behind. Worship becomes optional because he believes his future depends primarily on what he can accomplish. Without realizing it, he lives more like an orphan earning his place than a son receiving an inheritance.

He overcommits to appear capable.

He under-asks questions to avoid looking inexperienced.

His capital begins to move faster than his clarity—because when identity is unanchored, money becomes oxygen, and Johnny is beginning to breathe it.

FORMED JOHNNY

The money clears, but Johnny does not feel bigger. He feels entrusted. He remembers his father's quiet discipline. It was not flashy, not loud… just steady. And deeper still, he remembers something else: his father never defined himself by what he owned. He defined himself by what he built over time.

Johnny asks a different question: "Who was I before the wire transfer?" The answer does not change.

He is still a son.

He is still a friend.

He is still a man with strengths and blind spots.

He is still someone learning.

So one day each week, Johnny deliberately lays down the burden of producing. He gathers with God's people in worship, rests from his labor, and remembers whose he is. Sabbath is not an interruption to his calling; it is the weekly rehearsal of his identity. The Sabbath is the weekly refusal to live like an orphan. It reminds him that he belongs to the family of God and is a fellow heir with Christ. Because his inheritance is received rather than earned, he can rest without fear of falling behind.

His financial inheritance does not create identity. It reveals responsibility. When introduced in rooms of influence, he does not inflate.

He listens.

He asks questions without shame.

He says, "I'm still learning." And because his identity is rooted beneath performance, those words do not weaken him. They strengthen him.

When markets fluctuate, he does not panic, because his worth is not fluctuating. When others make larger moves, he does not rush, because comparison has lost its power.

He also does not upgrade his life to signal that he belongs, because belonging is never in question. When he gives—and he does give—it comes from settled abundance rather than the need to prove something.

Identity anchors him to the mountain. And because he can rest in his identity, access no longer feels like exposure—an imposter allowed in only because of the money, and one day certain to be found out. Rather, access feels like what it was always meant to be—stewardship.

STAGE III

Preparation

The Accumulation & Release Phases

What Is Being Formed Before the Avalanche Releases?

NOTHING that appears suddenly is ever truly unformed. Avalanches do not happen because snow merely exists; they form through a process of accumulation and change over time. Storms deposit fresh snow that settles and metamorphoses into layered snowpacks, with temperature variations, wind reshaping, and seasonal weather patterns influencing how those layers bond or weaken. Only when the internal structure becomes unstable under specific environmental conditions does the snowpack release what it has long carried.

Formation in the life of faith follows a similar rhythm. God rarely builds capacity through spectacle. He builds it in us through diligence and discernment. More often, he works through ordinary days, repeated choices, unseen disciplines, and steady obedience. What feels like stillness is frequently a season of construction.

This section explores how blessing accumulates before it ever moves. It looks at the environments, habits, and spiritual practices that build capacity. Preparation is not delay or divine indifference; it is protection, it is diligence. Snow builds one layer at a time. What is forming now will determine what can be carried later.

> *"Whoever is faithful in a very little is faithful also in much; and whoever is dishonest in a very little is dishonest also in much."*
> LUKE 16:10

4

Preparation That Precedes the First Divine Avalanche

In the mountains, avalanches are rarely born from a single storm. They emerge from long periods of hidden and unannounced accumulation—snowfall upon snowfall, layer upon layer, each deposit seemingly insignificant at the moment it falls. The landscape does not announce what it is becoming. Snow settles without spectacle. Weight gathers without drama. Only later, when movement finally comes, does the event appear sudden. Yet the accumulation was never sudden; it was forming all along.

The spiritual life often unfolds with the same hidden logic. Blessing rarely arrives out of nowhere. More often, it is the outcome of faithfulness practiced repeatedly in ordinary, unseen ways. Preparation rarely feels dramatic. It takes shape in habits, environments, and interior alignments that strengthen the heart long before circumstances shift. Much of what God builds is invisible at the time it is formed. In this way, blessing gathers like snow—not only through provision received, but through wisdom acquired, discipline sustained, and obedience lived across time.

This is why God never asks his people to wander blindly. It is the central thesis of this book, that he provides direction, rhythm, and structure for transformation, and then leads his people not only toward promise, but toward the kind of heart capable of receiving it. And by rhythm, what is meant is that God establishes habits that must be practiced with such consistency and patience that they eventually cease to feel like effort. They become simply how one lives. That is not mere behavior modification; that is transfiguration. That is the slow accumulation of formation—the spiritual snowfall that no one announces and few witness, yet without which no divine avalanche is possible.

Scripture and history both affirm this truth: the *conditions* we cultivate prepare us to receive what God provides. In other words, the environments we choose either prepare the heart for grace or resist it. The heart that has been ordered, practiced, and formed beneath the surface is the heart that can hold what suddenly arrives. The reason is rooted in the order of the Christian life: grace comes first, and our response follows. If that order is reversed, the disciplines become a way of trying to earn what God has already offered.

CONDITION 1: *Formation Under Pressure*

The Israelites offer a striking example of how preparation can continue even under severe limitation. In exile, they were cut off from land, political power, national security, and even the Temple, the center of their worship. By every visible measure, they had lost access. And yet, something unexpected happened. Rather than abandoning formation, they intensified it. Synagogues became centers of worship and learning. Literacy was preserved and valued. Torah study ordered daily life. Family traditions reinforced identity and continuity. Stewardship habits were taught intentionally across generations. These rhythms did not erase hardship. Exile was still exile. But they ensured that wisdom, discipline, and resilience continued to grow steadily, like snow accumulating on a mountain, even under pressure.

What was being built could not yet be seen… but it was being prepared.

Condition 2: *Rooted, Not Rushed*

Psalm 1 captures this dynamic with clarity and restraint:

> *"Happy are those who do not follow the advice of the wicked, or take the path that sinners tread, or sit in the seat of scoffers; but their delight is in the law of the Lord, and on his law they meditate day and night. They are like trees planted by streams of water, which yield their fruit in its season, and their leaves do not wither."*
>
> Psalm 1:1–3

Prosperity here is not sudden or shallow. It is the natural outcome of being rooted in the right environment over time. Growth happens in its season, not on demand. Fruit arrives because roots have been formed where nourishment is steady. This kind of preparation resists urgency. It values consistency over intensity and it trusts that what is planted faithfully will bear fruit when the time is right. The tree does not strain to produce fruit. Its strength comes from remaining connected to its source of nourishment. Season after season, the hidden work of rooting sustains the visible work of bearing fruit. In the same way, lasting provision grows from habits formed over time. What appears as abundance in one season is often the result of years spent cultivating stability, wisdom, and faithful stewardship.

CONDITION 3: *Preparation Is Protection*

Seasons of preparation rarely feel pleasant. They are often interpreted as delay, or worse, as punishment. Yet Scripture reveals a different reality: preparation is protection against being crushed by blessing.

> *"Now, discipline always seems painful rather than pleasant at the time, but later it yields the peaceful fruit of righteousness to those who have been trained by it."*
> HEBREWS 12:11

God does not prepare us because he is withholding blessing. He prepares us because blessing carries weight, and weight requires structure beneath it. Preparation through discipline shapes capacity. In other words, what we can safely receive depends on what we have been formed to carry. Two people may encounter the same provision, opportunity, or increase, yet experience vastly different outcomes because their interior structures differ.

Scripture repeatedly shows that God prepares people before entrusting them with what they will carry. Joseph's years of obscurity and imprisonment preceded the responsibility of stewarding Egypt's survival during famine (Genesis 41). Israel spent decades in the wilderness before entering the Promised Land, learning dependence, discipline, and covenant identity along the way (Deuteronomy 8). In both cases, preparation was not delay for its own sake; it was protection. What was coming required formation beforehand.

The saints repeatedly illuminate this hidden logic of formation. St. John of the Cross, in *Ascent of Mount Carmel* (I.13.11) describes how God frees the soul from attachments to prepare it for deeper union: "To come to possess all, desire the possession of nothing." He illustrates this journey through his well-known diagram of the "Mount of Perfection," where the narrow path to the summit is marked by a single word repeated again and again: *nada*—nothing. Every other path, though wider and more appealing, is lined with attachments, distractions, and lesser desires that cannot sustain the weight of divine union. Only the path of nada, the path of surrender and interior freedom, leads to the summit where God alone is enough. In the language of the avalanche, this same path becomes the channel through which blessing can safely descend.

What ascends through surrender
is what later returns without distortion.

The soul that has been cleared of excess can bear the weight of what comes. In this way, the path of nada is not loss, but preparation—the carving of a narrow, stable passage through which the fullness of God's provision can flow without burying the one who receives it. St. Francis de Sales brings a softer register to this same truth. In *Introduction to the Devout Life* (III.3), he counsels patience not only in the face of great trials, but in the smaller, daily irritations that tend to surround them—what might be called an active endurance, the kind that holds steady when nothing dramatic is happening and God's purposes are still unfolding out of sight. This theme runs deeply through the Catholic spiritual tradition.

Preparation, purification, delay, and unseen formation are repeatedly understood not as divine reluctance, but as mercy and protection.

Even outside theology, the same instinct surfaces. Chemist and microbiologist Louis Pasteur captured the heart of it in his 1854 inaugural address as Dean of the Faculty of Sciences at the University of Lille: "In the fields of observation, chance favors only the prepared mind." Pasteur saw that readiness, not luck, determines what we can receive.

However, some deep thinkers describe formation from the outside in. For instance, social psychologist Kurt Lewin, in *Principles of Topological Psychology*, developed what he called "Field Theory," arguing that human behavior cannot be understood by looking at personality or intention in isolation; it emerges from the dynamic interaction between the individual and the surrounding psychological environment. For Lewin, what surrounds us gradually shapes what we become. James Clear makes a similar observation in *Atomic Habits*: "You do not rise to the level of your goals. You fall to the level of your systems." Each of these captures something real—that preparation and structure shape outcomes. But they describe formation as environmental determinism, whereas Scripture points to something deeper: a preparation that is itself participation in God's sustaining grace, forming us from the inside out. Our disciplines do not manufacture that work.

Our disciplines are the ordinary means by which we cooperate with what God is already accomplishing within us.

In avalanche theology, this avoids both passivity ("God orders the natural systems that provoke the avalanche of blessing, so I do nothing") and self-reliance ("My disciplines transform me, therefore what I do becomes who I am"). Grace initiates. We cooperate. God gives the growth.

Like snow accumulating across seasons, this formation rarely announces itself while it is happening. By now, that hidden work is already underway. We have been granted access—drawn into covenant belonging—and we have begun to settle into identity, learning who we are before God when nothing has yet moved. These were interior movements, quiet and unseen. Preparation builds upon them as grace works through modest habits, repeated acts of trust, and faithful disciplines, gradually forming a life capable of sustaining what may later arrive. The work is subtle, yet its effects are decisive. What can eventually be received and faithfully carried is often determined long before movement becomes visible. These disciplines are not a means of gaining God's acceptance but a way of growing into the life he has already given. When we know we are loved, obedience becomes the grateful response of covenant rather than an anxious attempt to prove our worth.

CONDITION 4: *Prepared Ground*

In lived terms, prepared ground may include:

- ❄ *Layered snowpack with cohesion:* Gradual formation already underway, like habits of patience, discipline, and proportional thinking formed long before increase arrives.
- ❄ *Stable bedrock beneath accumulation:* Foundational beliefs about God and his promises regarding provision, security, and stewardship that lead to freedom from fear-driven or scarcity-conditioned thinking.
- ❄ *Deep root systems:* A life hidden with Christ that draws nourishment from prayer, Scripture, the sacraments, and communion with God's people rather than from changing circumstances.
- ❄ *Vegetation anchoring the slope:* Structures that prevent destabilization, like an identity rooted in Scripture rather than income, status, achievement, or external validation.
- ❄ *Natural drainage paths:* Mechanisms for processing emotional, spiritual, and psychological pressures, like a conversation with a trusted mentor, prayer, journaling, or other rhythms of discernment that give sudden

change somewhere to go before it overwhelms the person.

- *Established river channels:* Established habits for directing the daily flow of resources, like budgeting systems, donation frameworks, or saving routines that prevent reactive dispersion.
- *Strong riverbanks:* Clear boundaries that protect generosity, like the ability to say no, to delay commitments, to resist social pressure, and to prevent relational erosion.
- *Diversion channels and spillways:* Pre-decided allocations for directing overflow, like lending, almsgiving, charitable contributions, and long-term priorities established before abundance arrives.
- *Absorption capacity in the soil:* Steadiness under pressure—the ability to sit with uncertainty, discomfort, or sudden change without needing to immediately process it, talk about it, pray it away, or act on it.

CONDITION 5: *Choosing the Right Environment*

Yes, in the end, environment does matter. Change endures more readily when the environment supports it. Because the voices, habits, places, and rhythms we inhabit either reinforce or resist the work God is already doing within us, preparation includes intentionally choosing where we place ourselves and what we repeatedly allow to shape us. What we consistently see, hear, practice, and participate in slowly influences what we become. Belief precedes exposure, but repeated exposure either strengthens or weakens belief.

When someone chooses one faithful action each day, they are not merely completing a task; they are reinforcing identity. Large, sweeping plans trigger feelings of overwhelm, fear, and even procrastination because the nervous system reads them as threats. One small act, however, feels manageable, non-threatening, and repeatable, even on hard days. Ask yourself:

1) *"What voices am I regularly allowing to shape my thinking?"*

- A family member enthusiastically insisting, "Real estate always goes up—you'd be crazy not to buy now."
- A spouse reassuring, "Why worry about reserves? This opportunity may never come again."
- A colleague or friend observing, "Everyone who is successful leverages. Putting large sums down is just letting money sit idle."
- A peer group subtly reinforcing lifestyle expansion: "You work hard. You deserve to enjoy it."
- Social comparison whispering: "People will notice if you don't keep up."

2) *"What habits are shaping my reflexes?"*

- Scrolling social media each morning: Before prayer or Scripture, allowing comparison to set the emotional tone for the day.
- Making significant financial decisions impulsively: Acting before waiting, praying, or seeking wise counsel.

- ❄ Treating every increase in income as permission to increase spending: Instead of first asking how the increase might serve God's purposes.
- ❄ Reaching for reassurance before reflection: Constantly checking markets, account balances, or news feeds throughout the day, reinforcing anxiety rather than clarity.
- ❄ Normalizing urgency: Living in a state of perpetual "act now" thinking—flash sales, hot opportunities, fear of missing out—training the heart toward impulsive decision-making.
- ❄ Avoiding discomfort: Postponing difficult financial conversations, planning, or reviews, allowing short-term relief to override long-term stability.
- ❄ Expanding lifestyle automatically: Increasing spending in response to income increases without conscious evaluation, gradually redefining "normal" expenses.
- ❄ Outsourcing judgment: Relying excessively on opinions from friends, social media, commentators, or trends rather than cultivating internal discernment.
- ❄ Resisting deliberate pauses: Feeling compelled to decide immediately instead of embracing waiting, prayer, and discernment before major commitments.

3) *"What communities reinforce impulse rather than wisdom?"*

- ❄ Communities where comparison insidiously governs: Environments where spending, lifestyle, or visible success become measures of belonging, subtly pressuring members to keep up.

❄ Networks that normalize constant upgrading: Social circles where restraint feels abnormal and accumulation becomes the default expression of progress or achievement.
❄ Groups driven by urgency and hype: Spaces where decisions are framed as "now or never," discouraging reflection and rewarding rapid commitment.
❄ Echo chambers of optimism without risk awareness: Communities that celebrate opportunity but rarely discuss downside, fragility, or long-term consequences.
❄ Cultures of appearance over sustainability: Settings where visible signals of success receive affirmation while wisdom and patience remain invisible.

4) *"What rhythms anchor me when nothing dramatic is happening?"*
❄ Daily patterns that create steadiness: Consistent waking, working, resting, and sleeping rhythms that stabilize mood, energy, and judgment.
❄ Regular pauses for reflection: Moments intentionally reserved for stillness, prayer, journaling, or quiet thinking rather than constant stimulation.
❄ Financial check-in rituals: Calm, scheduled reviews of resources, spending, and obligations that prevent avoidance or reactive decision-making.
❄ Practices that reduce noise: Habits that limit informational overload and stepping back from news, markets, or social comparison cycles.
❄ Restorative routines: Activities that regulate the nervous system, like walking, praying, exercising.

What you repeatedly expose yourself to determines what accumulates within you, and what ultimately endures.

CLOSING REFLECTION

Snow builds without fanfare or announcement. But before we speak of building anything, we must remember what is already true: access has been granted, and our belonging is settled. We do not place ourselves in good soil to earn a place in God's family; we choose good soil because we already know whose we are. Formation begins not with effort but with belief—believing that the door is open, that we are known, that grace is already at work before we lift a finger.

Only from that settled place do the disciplines make sense.

Intentionally immerse yourself in environments that cultivate faith, clarity, and self-control—not to become someone you are not, but to make room for what God is already forming in you. Choose rhythms of study and prayer that reinforce truth. Surround yourself with people who practice discernment more than impulse, caution more than urgency.

These are not the means of earning blessing; they are how a settled heart cooperates with grace.

The aim is not striving, but formation. God performs the deep work as we remain faithful to the process. Snow never rushes to become an avalanche. It settles, layer upon layer, receiving what falls without striving to release it. The mountain does not force movement; it becomes ready for it.

Much of what God is forming in us follows this same unassuming pattern. The days that feel uneventful, the disciplines that feel small, the obedience that feels unseen—these are not interruptions to the story.

They *are* the story.

What feels like waiting is often weight gathering. What feels like delay is often hidden structure forming. And when the moment of movement finally comes, it will not be because something suddenly appeared, but because something long prepared is finally ready to be released.

Remember this above all: preparation is never the price of God's love; it is the response to it. Access always comes before preparation. Identity always comes before discipline. Because the door has already been opened through Christ, you are free to prepare—not to earn your place in God's family, but to live faithfully from it. Grace always initiates. We simply cooperate with what God is already doing. And in his perfect time, God himself brings the increase. Our task is not to manufacture the harvest, but to remain rooted, receptive, and faithful as he completes the work he has begun.

5

Abraham's Covenant: The First Divine Avalanche

When snow melts from the mountaintop, it does not choose to stop halfway down. It travels all the way into the valley, nourishing land it may never "see." In the same way, God's blessings are not meant only for us, but for those who come after us. The rivers of abundance are generational.

A powerful picture of this truth appears in God's covenant with Abraham:

> *"I will make of you a great nation, and I will bless you, and make your name great, so that you will be a blessing. I will bless those who bless you, and the one who curses you I will curse; and in you all the families of the earth shall be blessed."*
>
> GENESIS 12:2–3

Abram (later renamed Abraham) was seventy-five when God called him to leave everything familiar—his country, his kin, his father's household—and set out for a land he had never seen. It is important to note that Abraham and his nephew Lot were already prosperous before they ever left Haran. Scripture tells us Abraham was "very rich in livestock, in silver, and in gold" (Genesis 13:2). God's covenant, then, was not primarily about creating wealth; it was about ordering it, anchoring Abraham's life and resources in promise, and ensuring they would bless generations yet to come. God was not simply giving Abraham possessions; he was giving him an inheritance with purpose.

Pause with that for a moment. One of the least understood miracles in Abraham and Sarah's story is that God began stirring their "avalanche" late in life. Many of us assume our best years are behind us. But God does not measure time as we do:

> *"[W]ith the Lord one day is like a thousand years, and a thousand years are like one day."*
> 2 PETER 3:8

Why, then, does he wait?

Not out of indifference, but out of wisdom. Snow does not rush to the valley. It gathers layer upon layer, slowly, patiently, until the moment is right. The avalanche is not triggered by hurry but by ripeness. This does not mean we must grow old before God moves; only that he takes his time forming what he intends to release. Nothing accumulated in hidden seasons is wasted. When the time is ready, what has been gradually forming begins to move with the weight of God's faithfulness.

Abraham not only believed—he *moved.* Had he remained where he was, settled and safe in familiar surroundings, the story we all know and love might never have unfolded. Some avalanches begin only when we rise, take the first step, and follow God into the unknown. Abraham's story also mirrors the very pattern we have been exploring. Access preceded movement. Identity was reshaped before inheritance unfolded. Preparation stretched across decades before overflow appeared. What seems like a sudden miracle in Isaac was, in reality, the release of a long-forming accumulation.

God's call came with a promise: he would make Abraham a great nation, give him territory, and establish a lasting relationship. The covenant God made with Abraham would echo throughout Scripture. Again and again, God repeats the same relational promise:

> *"And you shall be my people, and I will be your God."*
> JEREMIAH 30:22

To seal this covenant, God made a solemn oath and later gave circumcision as its sign, marking Abraham's family as set apart for his purposes.

Still, the promise seemed impossible. Abraham and Sarah were elderly, and Sarah had been barren all her life. Years passed. They wrestled with doubt, longing, and misunderstanding, even trying to "solve" the promise through human effort by having a child through Hagar. Yet God returned repeatedly to reassure them: the covenant child would come through Sarah, by God's doing, not human strategy. God has a way of steadying those who walk with him. When the journey requires patience, he does not scold our questions; he meets them with reassurance and invites us to stay the course.

And when every natural hope had faded, God fulfilled his word. Sarah conceived and bore Isaac, whose Hebrew name means "laughter," because God had turned disbelief into astonishment and joy.

> *"Now Sarah said, 'God has brought laughter for me; everyone who hears will laugh with me.'"*
> GENESIS 21:6

Isaac became the living sign that God's covenant rests not on human strength but on divine faithfulness. He was the miracle child, the heir of the promise, through whom the covenant line would continue, ultimately pointing to Christ, the fulfillment of God's blessing to the nations. Isaac's birth reminds us that God's covenants unfold in his time and his way. What looked like delay was actually preparation. The covenant sealed with Abraham—land, people, blessing, and God's presence—flowed through Isaac like a river of meltwater moving from the mountain to the valley, carrying life into the generations that followed.

Obedience, however, did not bring Abraham instant arrival; it drew him into a lifelong pilgrimage of trust that reshaped his entire legacy. The promise was never meant for him alone. From the beginning, God designed his blessing to move beyond a single life to travel downward into generations yet unseen:

First, we have ABRAHAM (The snowfields, the avalanche, and the meltwater): In the language of the divine avalanche, Abraham is not merely someone who receives snow. He is the one upon whom the first great accumulation rests. His life becomes the slope upon which God begins building something that will one day move with immense force.

Before Isaac, before nations, before kings, there is Abraham standing under the weight of promise.

Layer by layer, trust is formed.

Layer by layer, covenant deepens.

Layer by layer, God builds what history will later experience as sudden.

When the long-awaited miracle finally arrives in Isaac, it appears as a dramatic release. Yet what seems abrupt is, in reality, the movement of what had been gathering for decades. Genesis hints at this enduring structure of blessing:

> *"I will bless those who bless you, and the one who curses you I will curse; and in you all the families of the earth shall be blessed."*
> GENESIS 12:3

God pronounces blessing not briefly, not accidentally, but intentionally. The promise is first carried, then released.

Then the channel of blessing arrived at ISAAC (the first valley; rooting; stabilization): Abraham's son inherited the covenant, and "like trees planted by streams of water, which yield their fruit in its season, and their leaves do not wither" ("Rooted, Not Rushed," pg. 117), the blessing became rooted and fruitful in Isaac. But Isaac is more than a recipient. He is the first proof that the avalanche does not end with the one who receives it.

Consider what Isaac does in a season of famine. When others flee, he stays. When the ground looks barren, he sows. And in the same year, in the very land where nothing seemed promising, he reaps a hundredfold.

> *"Isaac sowed seed in that land, and in the same year reaped a hundredfold. The Lord blessed him, and the man became rich; he prospered more and more until he became very wealthy."*
> GENESIS 26:12–13

Yet perhaps the most overlooked detail of Isaac's story is what he does with his father's wells. The Philistines had stopped them up, filling with earth what Abraham had carved with labor. Isaac returns to each one and re-digs them, restoring what envy had buried. He does not curse what was lost. He recovers it and then finds new living water beyond what his father had reached.

This is formation bearing fruit across generations. The meltwater does not simply vanish into the soil. It gathers beneath the surface, and Isaac learns to find it, to name it, and to draw from it. What Abraham accumulated through decades of trust, Isaac stabilizes through faithfulness practiced in ordinary, unglamorous acts: staying when others leave, planting when the season looks wrong, restoring what was stopped up, and seeking what was never before found.

The valley is not a passive place. It is where blessing becomes embedded in the land—where what came suddenly begins to sustain steadily.

Then came JACOB (the deeper valley; expansion through struggle): Isaac's son, Jacob, inherited the blessing, but his path to it was anything but smooth. He deceived, he fled, he labored, he was deceived in return. He wrestled with God through the night and refused to release his grip until blessing was secured. And yet this is not disqualifying. In the logic of the divine avalanche, Jacob's complexity is not a detour from formation. It *is* formation.

The valley the meltwater carves is not always clean and smooth. Sometimes it cuts through stone. Sometimes it floods and recedes before it finds its channel. Jacob's life is exactly that—blessing present but not yet settled; covenant expanding but not yet stable. God meets him in the disorder, nonetheless.

> *"And the Lord stood beside him and said, 'I am the Lord, the God of Abraham your father and the God of Isaac; the land on which you lie I will give to you and to your offspring; and your offspring shall be like the dust of the earth, and you shall spread abroad to the west and to the east and to the north and to the south; and all the families of the earth shall be blessed in you and in your offspring.'"*
>
> GENESIS 28:13–14

The promise is not diminished by Jacob's condition. It expands precisely *through* it. This is the deeper valley—not a place of failure, but a place of formation under pressure, where the covenant grows larger than any single lifetime can contain.

Then Jacob is renamed, ISRAEL (the river nations; transformed identity; multiplication): Jacob does not remain Jacob. After a night of wrestling at Peniel, God renames him Israel, *one who strives with God and prevails*, and the blessing enters an entirely new phase. This is not merely a change of name. It is a change of capacity. Jacob and Israel are not simply the same person at different ages. They represent two fundamentally different identities—and this book's central argument is that identity changes everything. Jacob is the striver, the one who schemes and wrestles and limps toward blessing. Israel is the one who has been broken open and renamed. His very capacity to carry the covenant has been transformed. The name change at Peniel is not incidental. It is the hinge. What Jacob carried by striving, Israel now carries by identity.

From Israel come twelve sons. From twelve sons come twelve tribes. From twelve tribes come kings, nations, prophecy, and ultimately Jesus Christ himself (Galatians 3:14)—the fulfillment of what God first spoke over a childless man standing under the stars.

"God said to him, 'Your name is Jacob; no longer shall you be called Jacob, but Israel shall be your name.' So he was called Israel. God said to him, 'I am God Almighty: be fruitful and multiply; a nation and a company of nations shall come from you, and kings shall spring from you.'"

GENESIS 35:10–11

"[I]n order that in Christ Jesus the blessing of Abraham might come to the Gentiles, so that we might receive the promise of the Spirit through faith."

GALATIANS 3:14

This is the valley reaching its full width. What began as one man's covenant has become a current of blessing that no single generation could contain—flowing outward and downward into peoples and centuries and eventually into every household that receives the Gospel. The avalanche that began with Abraham's trust has now become a lineage, a culture, a civilization, a promise embedded in history itself. The valley has become the world.

Scripture remembers God's covenant work through these three names—Abraham, Isaac, and Jacob (Israel). Yet avalanche theology is not a formula about timing, as if God only worked in predictable patterns of three. Yes, the triad can be found in the Scriptures to echo God's fullness or completeness, and to represent important cycles of transition. Yet it is a reminder that God's faithfulness stretches across generations. This is not timing magic but identity storytelling. If we are to ascribe any symbolism to the three names, perhaps it is safe to say that what begins in one life often finds its fullness in *children* and completeness in *grandchildren*, long after the first act of obedience (and let's not forget our spiritual sons and daughters, as well as communities of people we will never meet). Abraham never saw all these outcomes with his own eyes, yet his obedience set rivers in motion that flowed for millennia. His wealth was not just measured in livestock, silver, and gold, but in a generational covenant that still nourishes believers today.

Just as Abraham's obedience created rivers of blessing for generations, so too can our stewardship today create inheritance that nourishes our children's children, even in ways we may never see.

Which valley is receiving the rivers you are releasing today? You may be the Abraham in your family line: the first to obey, the first to steward, the first to believe beyond survival. You may never see the harvest, but heaven is already accounting for it.

Abraham stood at the summit of a promise
he would never fully see.
Yet the avalanche he trusted God would release...
is still moving through history today.

You, too, can stand at the summit of that same promise. The prayer that follows is an invitation to do exactly that.

Reader's Prayer: The Abrahamic Prayer

Lord, make me steady at the summit.
Form in me the unwavering courage of Abraham—
a willingness to release what I treasure most,
trusting that nothing entrusted to You is ever lost,
only transformed.
Let what You entrust to me keep moving.
Teach my heart to carry without fear.
Teach my hands to hold without grasping.
May resources never stagnate in my hands,
but flow where Your Spirit directs—
to heal, to build, to nourish, to restore,
never hardened by anxiety,
never stalled by control.
Whether the blessing flows through my own family,
or through the lives You weave into my story in ways I could
never predict, let those who come after me receive more life,
more wisdom, more faith.
And if I never live to see the deeper valley below,
let my obedience and steadiness still reach them.
Let unseen generations drink from wells I never drew from,
and walk in fields planted long before they arrived.
When You ask me to surrender,
grant me the grace to trust.
When You ask me to wait,
grant me patience without bitterness.
And when You release the avalanche,
grant me faith that remains when everything else passes away.
Amen.

6

How To Prepare the Heart

As we have seen, an avalanche may be powerful, but its impact is shaped by conditions hidden beneath the snow's surface. In avalanche science, what matters most is not the moment the snow begins to move, but everything that happens long beforehand Experts study the hidden structure of the *snowpack*: the layers of snow, how densely they are bonded, where weak layers form, and how pressure accumulates between them. They pay close attention to slope angle and places of tension where snow can either hold or fail. And they watch the conditions that stabilize or destabilize the snowpack over time: temperature shifts, wind, repeated storms, and subtle changes invisible to the untrained eye. Long before an avalanche ever occurs, its outcome is already being determined by what has been forming unseen beneath the surface.

This chapter focuses on the snow itself—the spiritual and mental preparation before gravity and a trigger propel the avalanche forward. Like snow gathering on a mountainside in silence, formation happens layer by layer: through prayer, discipline, awareness, surrender, and the ordering of the heart.

We have observed that in the natural world, an avalanche begins at the start zone, where accumulated snow rests under increasing pressure. When a hidden weak layer can no longer support the weight, the snow breaks free. It then moves rapidly down the track, gaining speed and force, until it reaches the runout zone, where it finally settles.

The same pattern exists within the soul. What accumulates within us—our thoughts, desires, attachments, habits, and beliefs—eventually reaches a point of movement. The question is not whether there will be movement, but whether what has formed can move without collapse, distortion, or destruction. Just as weak layers form within the snowpack long before the avalanche releases, so too must something give way within us before blessing can move. That something is *surrender.*

The Apostle Paul does not say God works around weakness. He says God works *through* it.

> *"My grace is sufficient for you, for power is made perfect in weakness."*
> 2 CORINTHIANS 12:9

The weak layer is not incidental to the avalanche. It is the mechanism of release. Without it, the snow never moves. The nutrients never reach the valley. The ecosystem never receives what it needs. The entire Beatitudes rest on this logic. *Blessed are the poor in spirit.*

Blessed are those who mourn. Blessed are the meek. The kingdom does not flow around weakness, but through it.

But if God moves through weakness, and weakness is the mechanism of release, then why prepare for abundance, and not simply remain weak and let God do what God does?

Weakness and disorder are not the same thing.

The weak layer in the snowpack is not chaotic snow. It is snow in a specific structural relationship to the layers above and below it, positioned in a way that allows for directional release. The avalanche flows because of the weak layer, but it flows toward the valley because the terrain has been shaped to receive it. Remove the weak layer and nothing moves. Remove the terrain—the rivers, the valleys, the root systems—and what moves destroys rather than nourishes.

Preparation is not the elimination of weakness. It is the ordering of it. God flows through poverty of spirit, through mourning, through meekness… what one may call *holy weaknesses*, surrendered and offered. But unpreparedness is not poverty of spirit. It is disorder. And disorder does not channel blessing; it scatters it. The unprepared heart does not possess more weakness than the formed heart; it possesses more unresolved chaos. Those unexamined fears, disordered attachments, and untested habits become the very things that overwhelm us instead of nourishing us. This is why sudden financial blessing requires preparation. Preparation transforms abundance into stewardship rather than collapse. The unformed heart believes blessing exists to secure the self, while the formed heart understands blessing exists to serve life beyond the self.

The snow phase is where that transformation begins. It is where the heart is prepared to carry weight, where identity is secured, and where hidden instability is revealed before pressure increases. What is formed here determines everything that follows: how we respond when opportunity comes, how we steward what is released, and whether what flows through our lives will nourish or overwhelm.

In the previous chapter, I intentionally set aside one central moment in Abraham's story—the sacrifice of Isaac. That omission was not accidental. The reason is simple:

Preparation always requires surrender.

And while Abraham's obedience is unmatched in scale, this posture of the heart can be compared to another figure in the Gospel of Luke: the widow with her two mites who gave everything she had.

At first glance, the comparison may seem disproportionate. How can the offering of two small coins be weighed alongside the surrender of a son? Yet God invites us to see something deeper. Though their gifts could not have been more different, their hearts were the same.

One offered pennies.

One offered an heir.

Both stood before God with open hands and complete trust.

Preparation, then, is not measured by the size of the sacrifice, but by the depth of surrender. It is this kind of surrendered heart that can carry the weight of blessing without being undone by it.

The early Christian tradition understood this truth well. St. Thomas Aquinas, drawing on St. Augustine, emphasized that the human heart must cooperate with God's grace rather than resist it: "*Qui creavit te sine te, non iustificabit te sine te*" ("He who created you without you will not justify you without you"; *Summa Theologiae,* I-II, q. 111, a. 2). Preparation, in this sense, is not the emptying of life but the opening of the hands, so that what God entrusts can land without destroying what receives it.

The widow in Luke's Gospel understood this instinctively. Though she possessed almost nothing, she refused to let fear close her hands. What little she held did not terminate in her grasp; it continued its movement toward God.

The Widow's Mite: *Small Gifts but Eternal Weight (Luke 21:1–4)*

Jesus watched as people placed offerings into the Temple treasury. Many wealthy worshipers contributed large sums. Then a "Certain Poor Widow" came forward and dropped in two small mites, almost nothing in the eyes of the world.

Jesus stopped everything:

> *"Truly I tell you, this poor widow has put in more than all of them; for all of them have contributed out of their abundance, but she out of her poverty has put in all she had to live on."*
> Luke 21:3–4

Biblical scholars note that a "mite" was a very small copper coin used in the time of Jesus. It was the smallest currency in circulation, the very lowest denomination. Two mites together were worth about one Roman quadrans, a tiny fraction of a day's wage. In practical terms, it was almost nothing, barely enough to buy a small amount of food. When the Certain Poor Widow dropped in two mites, she was not offering spare change. She was giving everything she had left. Others gave large amounts, but from their surplus. She, on the other hand, gave not from excess but from trust. Her offering did not change the Temple budget. It did not finance the ministry, nor did it impress anyone standing nearby.

But in heaven her offering carried eternal weight.

Her gift was not measured in currency but in surrender. Her offering became a declaration of trust: "God, *you* are my security." In that moment, the poor widow demonstrated the posture that prepares the heart to carry blessing. She did not allow fear to close her hands. Her story reminds us that preparation is not just about the size of the resource, but about the openness of the heart. Blessing cannot move through what is tightly held. The poor widow's offering flowed toward God rather than terminating in her grasp. Her story belongs here because she held nothing back, opening herself as a channel through which blessing could move—much like Abraham's surrender centuries earlier.

THE SACRIFICE OF ISAAC: *Trust That Costs Everything (Genesis 22)*

Long before the Certain Poor Widow, God promised Abraham a son—the son through whom the covenant would continue. Isaac represented future, promise, lineage, and blessing. Then came the unthinkable command:

> *"Take your son, your only son Isaac, whom you love, and go to the land of Moriah, and offer him there as a burnt offering…."*
> GENESIS 22:2

Abraham did not argue, bargain, or delay. He rose early, climbed the mountain, built the altar, and placed the most precious gift he had ever received into God's hands.

At the last moment, God intervened.

> *"Do not lay your hand on the boy or do anything to him; for now I know that you fear God, since you have not withheld your son, your only son, from me."*
> GENESIS 22:12

In that moment, Abraham discovered something he could not have known before: his heart belonged fully to God, not to the promise God had given. Because his heart was surrendered, blessing could expand rather than crush him. Wealth, lineage, legacy… none of it owned him. God did.

PREPARATION THROUGH THE HEART

When God asked Abraham for Isaac, he was not after the boy. He was after the heart.

And with the poor widow, God was not after the coins. He was after the heart.

One gift looked insignificant.

The other looked unbearable.

But heaven saw the same posture in both:

Nothing withheld.

Because Abraham's heart remained anchored in God, blessing flowed like rivers across generations. He became wealthy in cattle, silver, and gold; but more importantly, he became the spiritual ancestor of all who live by faith. And the poor widow—unseen, unnamed, and unnoticed—is remembered forever by Jesus himself. This is what Christ meant when he promised,

> *"Blessed are the poor in spirit, for theirs is the kingdom of heaven."*
> MATTHEW 5:3

To be poor in spirit is not merely to lack resources. A person can be materially poor and *not* be poor in spirit. It is a heart that knows, with deep confidence, that the Giver is greater than the gift.

Abraham could place Isaac on the altar because he trusted the Giver more than the promise.

The poor widow could surrender her last coins in the treasury because she trusted the Giver more than her security.

Heaven saw the same posture in both. And that is the kind of heart God prepares before blessing arrives—not a heart obsessed with accumulation, strategy, or control, but a heart that rests in a deeper freedom and confidently says: "I trust you more than the gift."

This insight is not new. The great spiritual traditions of the Church have long taught the primacy of God, the right ordering of affections, and the necessity of interior detachment. St. Ignatius of Loyola, in *Spiritual Exercises,* "Principle and Foundation" [23], cautions believers against clinging to created things for their own sake. The disciple must remain interiorly free—free to love, free to choose, and free to prefer God above every created good. Ignatian spirituality describes this freedom as holy indifference, not preferring wealth to poverty, health to sickness, or honor to dishonor, but desiring only what more fully leads to the end for which we are created: to know, love, and serve God. Similarly, St. Augustine described the spiritual life by making a careful distinction between created goods and God: God alone is to be enjoyed (*frui*) as a final end, and created goods are to be used (*uti*), received with gratitude but directed toward God rather than resting in them as though they were the destination (*On Christian Doctrine,* I.3–5). Augustine then deepens this through the concept of *ordo amoris* (ordered love) by stating that the just and holy life is one in which all things are loved in right order in reference to God, from whom all love finds its proper measure (*On Christian Doctrine,* I.27–28). St. Thomas Aquinas clarifies why the order matters. Created goods are real gifts, yet they are not self-sustaining. Only God is. Created goods are genuinely good, yet they are good by participation. God alone is good by essence (*Summa Theologiae,* I, q. 6, a. 3). Therefore, disorder enters when the human will rests in created gifts rather than in the divine source from which all goodness flows. The Church agrees in this same structure with pastoral simplicity: "Jesus enjoins his disciples to prefer him to everything and everyone…" (CCC 2544). More recently, in February of 2020, Pope Francis, in a general audience catechesis, emphasized that being poor in spirit is not something we achieve but an acknowledgment that "[w]e do not have to undergo any transformation because we already are! We are poor…" and that true interior freedom comes from knowing "how to love what is truly good more than [the self]."

AVALANCHE THEOLOGY AND ORDERED LOVE

While these streams of thought—poverty of spirit, detachment, ordered love, participation, and the avoidance of idolatry—share the same underlying structure, avalanche theology does not propose a new doctrine. Rather, it rearticulates this perennial Christian wisdom through the relational distinction between the Giver and the gift, particularly within the experienced tensions of abundance, stewardship, and psychological formation.

The Beatitudes, particularly the call to be poor in spirit, have historically been understood within this same framework. Poverty of spirit does not imply the absence of gifts, but freedom from enslavement to them. In the Ignatian tradition, this freedom is described as interior detachment—not a coldness toward created things, but an ordering of the heart so that no created good, whether status, security, wealth, or comfort, holds a claim that belongs to God alone. The soul that is interiorly free is not indifferent to life; it is free to love rightly, to receive gratefully, and to release without grasping. This is the interior condition that prepares the heart to carry blessing without being ruled by it.

To prepare for God's divine avalanche, the believer must grasp the vital mind-heart connection:

Love the Giver more than the gifts, because gifts without relationship can easily become burdens.

This is not a warning against receiving. It is an explanation of what happens when gifts arrive without the relationship that teaches us how to hold them. A gift received without identity becomes a source of confusion. The recipient no longer knows who they are apart from what they have. A gift received without wisdom becomes a source of pressure: every decision feels irreversible; every relationship becomes suspect. A gift that replaces the Giver in the heart becomes the heaviest burden of all, tasked with doing what it was never designed to do—provide unconditional love, lasting peace, and the answer to meaning. When we expect gifts to do what only the Giver can do, they collapse under the weight of that demand, and so do we.

In every case, the burden is not the gift itself. The burden is the absence of the relationship with the Giver who would have taught the recipient how to hold the gift rightly. This is why formation must precede provision.

The Giver forms us for the gift before he releases it, not because he is withholding, but because he is protecting us from being crushed by what he intends to bestow.

This love remains steadfast whether God grants abundance or withholds it, whether his providence is readily understood or deeply mysterious. It is the posture of one who loves God not merely for what he gives but for who he is, trusting him whether his ways console or unsettle, whether his designs are clear or concealed.

Moving Forward

In the pages ahead, we will ask what it means to cultivate that kind of heart—the heart that can receive without clinging, give without fear, steward without being ruled, and surrender without knowing the outcome.

For the surrendered heart, the avalanche is not dangerous; it becomes an unburdened gift.

It becomes meltwater.
It becomes rivers.
It becomes life.

Prepare Spiritually:

Anchor Your Heart in God

Before anything else, the heart must be ready. Wealth magnifies what already lives within us: gratitude or greed, insecurity or confidence, humility or pride. Anchoring the heart in God means rooting your identity, desires, and decisions in his truth so that circumstances cannot shift who you are or how you respond.

> *"But strive first for the kingdom of God and his righteousness, and all these things will be given to you as well."*
> Matthew 6:33

> *"As for those who in the present age are rich, command them not to be haughty, or to set their hopes on the uncertainty of riches, but rather on God who richly provides us with everything for our enjoyment."*
> 1 Timothy 6:17

> *"Keep your heart with all vigilance, for from it flow the springs of life."*
> Proverbs 4:23

PRACTICAL APPLICATION: Preparing Spiritually with the **AVALANCHE EXAMEN**

It is time to anchor your life in the Giver rather than the gift. Growth requires space—space for the imagination to perceive what God is forming within us.

In the tradition of Ignatian spirituality, an Examen is a simple prayer of reflection that helps us notice where God is present and how our hearts are being formed. This practice is not done alone without help. From the beginning, the Holy Spirit is the guide of the journey—helping us see what is hidden, interpret what is forming, and respond in truth and freedom (John 16:13). Traditionally practiced at the end of each day, the Examen invites us to recognize where God has been at work throughout the day and how we have responded. Rather than evaluating success or failure, it cultivates a deeper attentiveness to God's ongoing work in our lives.

Ignatius structured it around five simple movements:

1) Begin with gratitude, thanking God for the gifts and graces of the day.
2) Review the day in God's presence, asking where he was at work and where you noticed his invitations.
3) Notice with honesty where you experienced consolation or desolation—moments of peace, joy, and closeness to God, as well as moments of restlessness, temptation, or distance.
4) Respond in repentance and trust, bringing both your failures and your desires for growth before the Lord, receiving his mercy.

5) Finally, look forward to tomorrow in hope, asking for the grace, wisdom, and strength to walk faithfully in the day ahead.

What follows is a guided adaptation—an Avalanche Examen—designed to help you review your financial life in the presence of the Holy Spirit by recognizing what is steadily accumulating beneath the surface.

While the Avalanche Examen can be used to examine individual transactions or outcomes, try to notice the deeper patterns of formation, stewardship, and provision that are unfolding over time. While the Ignatian Examen is traditionally prayed each evening, the Avalanche Examen can be practiced weekly, monthly, or whenever you want to reflect more intentionally on significant financial decisions and the direction they are shaping. Do not worry about fully understanding the AIPOM framework at this point. The terms simply serve as guideposts, helping you become more attentive to God's work and your response.

Find a quiet place, become still before the Lord, and ask the Holy Spirit for guidance into the following reflections:

1) Begin with gratitude for the snow.

Close your eyes. Take a slow breath. You are standing at the summit, in the start zone, where the snow has been gathering around you.

Begin by naming three gifts you did not create: your breath, your heartbeat, the warmth of the sun, the sound of birds, the love of a pet, the simple fact that you woke up this morning. Do not rush. Let each one settle before moving to the next. Now consider the ways God has provided for you today. What resources, opportunities, or relationships supported you? Where did you experience enough for today? Did you receive a paycheck, complete meaningful work, enjoy a meal, use reliable transportation, or benefit from someone's generosity? Even in a difficult season, where can you recognize God's provision in the ordinary moments of your financial life?

In avalanche science, snow does not fall all at once. It accumulates layer by layer, flake by flake, over an entire season. What eventually releases as an avalanche began as something almost imperceptible—a single snowflake, then another, then another, each one settling onto what came before. No single flake decides the moment of release. But every flake matters. This is where we begin: not with striving, but with receiving.

Gratitude is the first snowfall that begins to accumulate upon the foundation of God's grace. It trains the heart to recognize that access to God's provision is not something we earn; it is something we receive, much like the welcome we experienced at grandmother's house, where our place was already prepared before we arrived. Each act of thanksgiving acknowledges that we are already standing on ground we did not build, breathing air we did not create, and held by a covenant we did not initiate. Each gift you name becomes another layer of snow settling into the start zone. Over time, the snowpack becomes a life of accumulated trust, formation, and faithful stewardship.

This is how access begins—not by forcing your way in, but by recognizing that the door was already open, that you were already expected, that your place was already prepared. Nothing reorders the heart more quickly than this: the recognition that grace has already been at work long before you arrived.

Rest here for a moment. The snow is settling. When you are ready, move to Step 2.

2) Review where God was at work beneath the surface.

You are still at the summit with your eyes closed, standing in the start zone. The snow has settled from Step 1. Now imagine looking down. Beneath your feet, well beneath the surface, layers have been forming that you cannot see from above.

Ask God one question and then listen: "Lord, where were you today, and how did I respond?" Do not rush to answer. Let what surfaces come on its own. Now consider the hidden movements within your financial life. What decision, conversation, purchase, act of generosity, or moment of restraint revealed something about your heart? Where did you sense God's invitation to trust him more deeply? Did you respond with peace, fear, contentment, anxiety, wisdom, or haste?

In avalanche science, the most important information about a snowpack is rarely visible from the surface. Beneath what appears calm and undisturbed, layers are forming and bonding—or failing to bond. Some layers are strong and load-bearing. Others are weak, hollow, waiting for pressure to reveal them. The trained eye learns to read what is happening beneath the surface before the mountain moves. Formation happens long before it becomes visible in our choices. For this reason, both an avalanche instructor and a spiritual director might caution that stability is never assumed; it is examined.

This is the work of identity. At grandmother's house, you did not have to earn your seat at the table before receiving the meal. You belonged before you contributed. You were welcomed before you performed. In the same way, God's covenant teaches us to make financial decisions from the security of belonging rather than from fear, comparison, or the need to prove our worth. As you reflect on your day, ask not only what you did with your resources, but who you believed yourself to be while doing it. While Access asks, "What has God entrusted to me today?" Identity asks, "Who was I while I managed what he entrusted to me?" Did your choices flow from the confidence of being God's beloved child on the mountain of covenant? Or were they driven by anxiety, scarcity, status, or the need for approval? Many disordered financial behaviors begin long before a purchase is made or a budget is ignored.

Much of the financial disorder begins with a forgotten identity.

Returning to your true identity in Christ allows stewardship to flow from trust instead of striving. As you return to this practice day after day, you begin to recognize what draws you closer to God, what pulls you away, where you experienced peace, and where pressure exposed places that still need healing. Keep a small journal nearby. Note what returns over time—the nudges, the Scriptures, the recurring patterns, the moments when fear replaced trust, and the gentle reminders of your true identity in Christ.

These are the hidden layers of your snowpack. Some patterns will strengthen what is forming. Others will need attention before pressure increases and movement begins.

Rest here for a moment. You have seen what is beneath the surface. When you are ready, move to Step 3.

3) Allow the Holy Spirit to reveal what creates peace and trust (consolation) and what creates chaos and runoff (desolation).

You are still at the summit. If you journaled, close your eyes again. You are beginning to see the patterns beneath the surface more clearly. What was accumulating in silence is now becoming visible through diligence and discernment. This is the moment the hidden layers are brought into the light and what is disordered begins to be revealed.

Ask the Holy Spirit: "Where did I experience trust and peace today—and where did status, approval, fear, control, or comparison begin to shape my decisions?" Do not rush to answer. Name what surfaces. Write it down. Do not rush to fix it. Simply let it stand in God's presence.

In avalanche science, there is a careful distinction that bears repeating. The weak layer in the snowpack is not chaos. It is the mechanism through which the mountain releases what has been building. Likewise, weakness surrendered to God becomes the very place where movement begins. The Beatitudes rest on this logic. *Blessed are the poor in spirit. Blessed are those who mourn.*

As mentioned earlier, God moves through holy weakness, not around it.

But disordered attachments are something different. They are not weak layers. They are unexamined fears, misplaced trust, and competing loyalties that have never been brought into the light. Examples of disordered attachments might include needing a certain income level to feel worthy or respected, or hoarding cash beyond reasonable reserves because scarcity feels permanent, or micromanaging family members' spending as a form of relational control. In an avalanche, these are the hidden instabilities that cause the snowpack to fracture unpredictably, sending snow sideways and every which way, scattering across the slope in chaos and into runoff. This is why diligence and discernment are both needed to uncover the disordered attachments. Left hidden, these attachments do not channel blessing. They scatter it.

This is why we invite the Holy Spirit into our avalanche rehearsal—into the "dry run" of the avalanche just before the slab releases, before it travels down the track, and before it reaches the runout zone. What is named here can be guided into established paths and channels. What remains hidden continues to contribute to the disorder and the chaos.

This is Preparation. While Access asks, "What has God entrusted to me today?" and Identity asks, "Who was I while I managed what he entrusted to me?" Preparation asks, "What in me is ordered, and what remains disordered?" What moves through you next depends on what you allow the Spirit to see now.

Rest here for a moment. You are now seeing more clearly what has been forming beneath the surface. You have examined the difference between weak layers that form surrendered weakness and grace-enabled transformation, and disordered attachments that amount to hidden instability and fragmentation of stewardship. When you are ready, move to Step 4.

4) Surrender what has been revealed and discern where it is meant to flow.

Eyes still closed, imagine the divine avalanche has occurred and reached the runout zone. The snow has stopped moving. What was racing down the mountain has finally settled—tons of accumulated formation now resting at the base of the slope. What happens next will depend on your surrender and forward discernment.

Take what the Spirit revealed in Step 3—the trust and the peace, as well as the attachments, fears, and competing loyalties—and place them before the Lord. Release them in prayer: "Lord, I thank you for the places where your grace was at work today. I surrender the places I cannot govern rightly. Teach me to hold everything—both gifts and burdens—with open hands." Now ask for forward discernment: "Lord, what is this for, and where does it belong? Show me what leads to life and what only appears to be movement." This step hinges upon the knowledge that not everything that moves is guidance and not everything that flows is life-giving. In this stage of the journey, provision becomes water, and water must be guided. Not every movement is direction. Not every open path leads to life. What feels like momentum may still require restraint, and what feels like urgency may not be calling.

This is Opportunity. The divine avalanche has landed. Now judgment is tested. What was formed in diligence must now be directed with discernment. Water that is guided becomes a river that nourishes the valley below. Water without direction becomes runoff and is lost.

Diligence formed what you now hold.

Surrender clears what cannot be carried forward.

Discernment guides what should flow and where it is meant to go.

While Access asks, "What has God entrusted to me today?" and Identity asks, "Who was I while I managed what he entrusted to me?" and Preparation asks, "What in me is ordered, and what remains disordered?" Opportunity asks: "What should I surrender, and what should I send forward?"

Rest here for a moment. Keep journaling if necessary. The snow is melting into life-giving water that will eventually flow downhill into the valley. When you are ready, follow it to Step 5.

5) Release forward grace and nourish the valley.

Eyes still closed, imagine the avalanche has completed its journey and the water is moving through the landscape now, seeping into the soil, reaching places the snow could never have touched while it was still frozen on the mountain.

Begin by imagining yourself in a moment of unexpected abundance. The imagination, when trained toward generosity, begins to shape the will before the moment of decision ever arrives. Ask God one question:

"Lord, who is in my valley?" Let names and faces surface: a person, a family, a community, a cause. Do not rush and do not edit what comes. Simply receive it. Then ask a second question, this one about motive: "Am I giving to be seen, or to be faithful?"

In avalanche science, meltwater does not stay where it lands. It moves. It permeates. It nourishes root systems, fills riverbeds, and sustains ecosystems far beyond the point where the snow first fell. What began as a single snowflake at the summit has traveled the entire length of the mountain and is now doing its most important work in the valley below. This is what grace does when it is released rather than held.

Jesus speaks directly to this in the Sermon on the Mount. Generosity offered without recognition—to strangers, to the poor, to the vulnerable, without applause or audience—is one of the clearest signs that the heart is becoming rightly ordered toward God. As Christ teaches: "[W]hen you give alms, do not let your left hand know what your right hand is doing" (Matthew 6:3). Begin small. Formation does not require scale; it requires willingness. Those who are faithful in little are entrusted with more. Each hidden act of generosity becomes part of a larger movement of grace, nourishing lives beyond what you can see, reaching generations you will never meet.

This is the valley, where blessing was always headed. This is Multiplication. The snow that gathered at the summit has completed its journey. While Opportunity asks: "What should I surrender, and what should I send forward?" Multiplication asks: "Whom is God calling me to nourish in the valley?"

Rest here. Then carry what has been entrusted into the day ahead.

Prepare Mentally:

To Steward, Not Fear

Scripture does not divide the heart from the mind. The biblical heart is the whole interior person—intellect, will, and affection together—the hidden center where a life is actually decided. To prepare the heart is to prepare the mind. What follows continues the work of the previous pages. It reaches the faculty that decides.

These practices work differently than the Avalanche Examen. An examen is a guided exercise, something you can complete in a single sitting, alone or with a group in the stillness of a morning. These cannot be completed. They are disciplines to inhabit, built slowly over seasons into the ordinary structure of daily life.

Mental preparation forms the inner structure that supports what accumulates. It steadies the heart so that increase meets discernment rather than impulse. In the Snow Phase, the mind is trained to see clearly and to resist the urgency that often accompanies provision.

Fear rushes; wisdom waits.

This kind of formation does not happen in the moment of pressure. It is built beforehand, layer by layer, through disciplined thought and honest reflection. When the weight of increase arrives, the prepared mind does not panic; it recognizes, orders, and directs what has been given.

> *"The beginning of wisdom is this: Get wisdom, and whatever else you get, get insight."*
> PROVERBS 4:7

> *"If any of you is lacking in wisdom, ask God, who gives to all generously and ungrudgingly, and it will be given you."*
> JAMES 1:5

> *"For which of you, intending to build a tower, does not first sit down and estimate the cost, to see whether he has enough to complete it?"*
> LUKE 14:28

The following three formative disciplines are monastic traditions reframed for the terrain of sudden abundance. In avalanche theology, this is how the snowpack is formed, bonded, and tested under pressure long before any release occurs.

I. ASCETICISM is the practice of self-control. Like compacting the snow so that what accumulates can bear weight without collapse, Asceticism strengthens the soul to carry what God entrusts without fracturing under pressure. At its heart, Asceticism asks a simple question: Can you control yourself when abundance suddenly arrives?

Though its roots can be traced to earlier philosophical traditions, Asceticism became more clearly defined within the early centuries of Christianity as the Church began to articulate practices that formed the soul. Between the first and third centuries, early Christians embraced rhythms of fasting, prayer, simplicity, and self-denial as a way of following Christ more closely. By the third and fourth centuries, the Desert Fathers and Mothers (figures such as St. Anthony of Egypt and Amma Syncletica of Alexandria) gave these practices more intentional shape, withdrawing into the Egyptian desert to pursue lives of prayer, detachment, and spiritual clarity. These early traditions were preserved and transmitted to later generations through the writings of John Cassian, a Latin-writing monk from the Balkans who spent years living among the Desert Fathers and recorded their practices in *The Institutes* (c. AD 420), a work that later influenced St. Benedict of Nursia and Western monasticism. By the fourth through sixth centuries, Asceticism was further structured within emerging monastic communities.

In order to practice self-control, we must bring hidden patterns, fears, and desires into the light so they no longer govern us unconsciously. It is about freedom—freedom from what secretly rules the heart. In the accumulation phase, Asceticism forms the layers of the soul, shaping what is building beneath the surface long before any pressure is felt.

Formation happens over time. Each experience, belief, and habit settles like a layer in the snowpack. Some layers bond and strengthen the structure. Others remain weak, hidden beneath the surface, waiting for pressure to reveal them. Asceticism allows us to see these layers clearly, to strengthen what can bear weight, and to address what cannot. For example:

1) SELF-KNOWLEDGE: *Name your money stories.*

Ask yourself: "What did I learn about money growing up?"

Self-control begins with self-knowledge. We cannot order what we have not yet seen. What remains unnamed retains silent control. What is brought into the light begins to lose its power.

Childhood is often where our deepest financial fears first take root, like scarcity, instability, silence, shame, or pressure. Take time to inventory the moments that left a mark: the seasons, stories, or events where money, or the lack of it, shaped your sense of security or worth. Write them down.

2) SELF-CORRECTION: *Learn from your mistakes without shame.*

Instead of saying, "I failed," say, "I discovered a weak spot, and now I will strengthen it."

Shame paralyzes; wisdom observes, learns, and reframes. Formation comes from meeting failure honestly and seeing where structure cannot yet bear weight. The ascetic response to failure is honest examination followed by deliberate correction.

3) SELF-DIRECTION: *Train your imagination toward stewardship, not fantasy.*

Instead of imagining only what money could buy, begin asking:

❄ What could this sustain?
❄ Whom could this bless?
❄ What could this build?

The imagination, when untrained, fuels consumption. When formed, it becomes a tool for stewardship, shaping how future increase will be received and directed. The imagination is precisely what Classical Asceticism targets—the interior faculty that generates desire before the will ever engages. Ignatius called this the "composition of place." The Desert Fathers had a name for the restless inner thoughts that precede and generate temptation: *logismoi*. In the *Praktikos*, the fourth-century desert monk Evagrius Ponticus identified eight of them; Cassian later carried the scheme into the Latin West as the eight principal vices.

4) SELF-ORDERING: *Treat money as a servant, never a savior.*

This discipline connects directly to the classical ascetic goal of right ordering—ensuring that created goods serve rather than rule. When money begins to claim identity, security, or worth, remind yourself: "Money can serve my calling. It cannot be my calling."

This principle extends further than we might expect. Money and artificial intelligence are among the most powerful tools available to us today—and both make excellent servants but terrible masters. Each can extend human capacity, multiply resources, and serve genuine good. Each can also, when trusted beyond its proper role, gradually reshape the heart around its own logic. What we trust shapes how we live. Asceticism restores right order to that trust, ensuring that what accumulates—whether wealth, technology, or influence—does not distort the heart it was meant to serve.

II. PRUDENCE is the practice of wisdom. It teaches us to see clearly and judge rightly, like reading the slope and conditions before taking a step—discerning what is stable, what is shifting, and when movement should or should not occur. At its heart, Prudence asks a simple question: Can you make wise decisions when abundance suddenly expands your options?

Like Asceticism, Prudence did not emerge at a single moment but developed through both philosophical reflection and theological insight. In the ancient Greek world, philosophers such as Plato and Aristotle described Prudence (*Phronesis*) as the capacity to discern the right course of action in concrete situations. It was not merely knowledge, but the disciplined ability to perceive reality clearly and respond wisely, especially under changing conditions and increasing pressure. In *The Four Cardinal Virtues*, the twentieth-century Catholic philosopher Josef Pieper explains how Christianity embraced and deepened this classical understanding, recognizing Prudence as the virtue that rightly perceives reality and directs moral action. Prudence became one of the four cardinal virtues, alongside Justice (fairness), Temperance (moderation), and Fortitude (courage). It orders decision-making, guiding when to act, when to wait, and how to move in alignment with truth. Like reading the slope before taking a step, Prudence teaches us to see clearly, judge wisely, and recognize when conditions are stable enough to move.

In the accumulation and release phase, Prudence evaluates the condition of what has formed. It recognizes pressure, identifies risk, and resists premature movement. Where Asceticism forms the layers, Prudence discerns whether those layers can bear weight. For example:

1) DISCERNMENT: *Replace panic-thinking with planning-thinking.*

When new money comes in, pause. Breathe. Do not react. Sudden provision often introduces pressure—urgency, excitement, or fear. Wisdom resists impulsive movement, recognizing that reaction can trigger instability before structure is ready.

> *"The plans of the diligent lead surely to abundance, but everyone who is hasty comes only to want."*
> PROVERBS 21:5

Wisdom often looks ordinary:

- Paying off high-interest debt
- Building an emergency reserve
- Choosing stability over spectacle

These decisions create margin, and margin is what allows future increase to be carried without strain.

2) PATIENCE: *Practice delayed decisions.*

When something feels urgent, wait twenty-four to forty-eight hours. This discipline trains the mind to resist pressure and recognize that money is not your master, God is.

3) COUNSEL: *Normalize professional advice.*

Seek wisdom before making significant decisions. Consult a financial professional, attorney, or qualified advisor. Isolation magnifies blind spots; counsel exposes them before they become points of failure.

4) VISION: *Think in decades, not moments.*

Ask:

- ❄ What will matter in ten years?
- ❄ What would faithfulness look like over a lifetime?
- ❄ What kind of legacy do I want this resource to support?

Stewardship requires a long horizon. Prudence stretches the mind beyond impulse into vision, ensuring that decisions are made from stability, not under pressure. The prepared mind does not panic when the slab begins to move. It reads the conditions, chooses the moment, and steps with wisdom rather than fear.

III. A RULE OF LIFE is the practice of ordered daily living. It establishes rhythms and structures that create channels and guardrails, directing what flows into our lives rather than allowing it to become dispersed. At its heart, a Rule of Life asks a simple question: Will your daily rhythms remain faithful when abundance suddenly changes your life?

Like Asceticism and Prudence, a Rule of Life did not emerge at a single moment but took recognizable shape within early Christian monastic communities between the third and sixth centuries.

As believers sought to live with greater intentionality, especially in the deserts of Egypt and Syria, spiritual leaders began organizing daily rhythms of prayer, work, rest, and community life. These patterns were eventually written down as "rules," not as rigid laws, but as guides for living faithfully and consistently. One of the most influential expressions came in the sixth century through the Rule of St. Benedict—the foundation of Western monasticism and the origin of what most people today mean when they talk about a Rule of Life. Earlier monastic rules had been extremely severe. There were long fasts, minimal sleep, and harsh penances. Benedict deliberately softened these extremes, writing what he called "a little rule for beginners" that was sustainable for ordinary human beings living in community rather than heroic ascetics living alone in a desert.

Over time, the idea of a Rule of Life extended beyond monasteries, becoming a practical framework for anyone seeking to order life around what matters most. At its core, a Rule of Life is simply a set of intentional rhythms and practices that create stability, strengthen structure, and prepare a life to receive what it has not yet encountered. In the accumulation phase, a Rule of Life prepares the structure, building the channels that will carry blessing toward the valley when the season turns. For example:

1) PROTECTION: *Create pre-decided rules of safety.*

A pre-decided rule of safety removes the need to deliberate when pressure arrives. What is decided in advance cannot be undone by urgency, fear, or excitement in the moment. Examples of rules of safety:

❄ Allow no major financial decisions under emotional stress.
❄ Structure generosity; giving is planned in advance.
❄ Save consistently; saving is automatic.
❄ Ensure basic protections (insurance, legal clarity, beneficiaries, estate planning).

2) FORMATION: *Read Scripture through the lens of formation, not fortune.*

Ask yourself: "What is this teaching me about trust, patience, and wisdom?"

This anchors the mind in truth and protects the heart from the distortion when pressure and provision arrive.

3) VIGILANCE: *Establish fixed rhythms of review.*

What is not revisited tends to drift. Create regular moments—weekly, monthly, annually—to review your resources, decisions, and direction. These are moments of alignment, not anxiety.

Ask:

❄ Where is pressure increasing?
❄ Where is structure holding firm?
❄ Where is the structure weakening?
❄ Where is God inviting adjustment?

Like a mountain observed over time, stability is maintained by attending to small shifts before they become large failures.

4) Order: *Pre-decide your allocation priorities.*

Do not wait until abundance arrives to decide what it is for. The channels should be clear before the meltwater flows. Establish clear categories that reflect your values:

- ❄ What portion is for God (first fruits)?
- ❄ What portion is for protection (reserves)?
- ❄ What portion is for growth (investment or building)?
- ❄ What portion is for generosity and enjoyment?

This is *ordo amoris* (p.149) made practical by the Rule of Life. Every resource is directed toward its proper end. When these channels are defined ahead of time, decisions are made from clarity; structure is strengthened before pressure arrives.

Closing Reflection

When the heart is surrendered and the mind is steady, abundance becomes something we can receive and steward with clarity. Preparation is rarely dramatic. It happens in the stillness of ordinary days, in the small decisions to trust God, to give, to plan with wisdom before pressure arrives. These choices may seem insignificant in the moment, yet they shape the inner terrain long before blessing ever arrives.

Like the hidden layers of a snowpack forming high on a mountain, the structures of the heart are built slowly, over time.

Gratitude deepens humility.
Generosity loosens the grip of fear.
Wisdom steadies the mind.

And a steadied mind is how the heart learns to hold what God entrusts.

When the heart has learned to love the Giver more than the gifts, abundance no longer threatens to bury us.

And when the heart has been prepared in this way, opportunity arrives as stewardship.

Reader's Prayer:
Spiritual and Mental Anchoring

Lord, today I honor You and give thanks.
I acknowledge that I have not always stewarded Your blessings with wisdom or care.
Too often, what has come into my hands has quickly passed through them.
I have chosen impulse over discernment,
urgency over patience, and consumption over preparation.
Yet even in my shortcomings,
You have been patient with me,
teaching, shaping, and forming my heart.
I thank You for Your mercy, Your instruction,
and Your unwavering grace.
You remind me that I am Your beloved,
that what You entrust to me is not meant to overwhelm me, but to flow through me for Your purposes.
So today, I offer myself again—
my heart, my mind, and my will.
Order my desires.
Clarify my thinking.
Teach me to recognize what is forming within me,
to release what I am holding too tightly,
and to receive what You give with humility and readiness.
Form in me a heart that trusts the Giver more than the gifts, a mind that chooses wisdom over impulse,
and a life that reflects Your order rather than my fears.
Prepare me, Lord, for what You are building—so that when the moment of movement comes, I will be ready to receive it without fear and steward it without confusion.
Amen.

7

Practical Readiness: Preparing the Terrain Before the Avalanche Releases

In avalanche country, most avalanches that kill people are triggered by the victims themselves. This is why backcountry skiers and mountaineers study the *terrain* before they ever set foot on a slope. They measure slope angles with inclinometers, looking for the critical range between thirty and forty-five degrees where instability is greatest. They identify anchors—trees, rock bands, and ridgelines. They read the terrain for convexities and terrain traps that shape how weight is distributed. They look for gullies and bowls where even a small slide can become fatal. They do not study the terrain because they are afraid of the mountain. They study it because they respect what it carries.

We, too, must prepare for what happens when what has been forming is finally set in motion. The blessing is not the danger. The danger is entering the terrain unprepared and triggering the very collapse we could have avoided.

If the terrain below is weak or untested, release brings destruction. But if the structures have already been shaped by previous experience, by formation, by channels carved through faithfulness, what is released moves with integrity rather than chaos. What is not structured before release will fracture under it. What is not ordered in stillness will be exposed in motion.

Up to now, we have examined the heart and studied the snowpack. Now we turn to what happens when accumulation of snow reaches its tipping point. God's blessings are real, and so are the responsibilities that accompany them. Preparation is spiritual, mental, and thoroughly practical. What has formed within must now be supported by what is built around us.

Consider what you have already done:

❄ You distinguished identity from access.
❄ You studied your environment and learned that belief precedes exposure to it.
❄ You examined the movements of the heart with an Avalanche Examen.
❄ You built the interior disciplines that steady the heart: Asceticism, Prudence, and a Rule of Life.

Now the question becomes: Will what you have built hold when movement begins?

The practical work of readiness means preparing your life financially and relationally so that when blessing is released, your life can carry it with purpose.

This is the final stage before movement.

This is where the terrain decides whether it will hold… or give way.

PREPARE FINANCIALLY:
AVALANCHES PREFER PRE-EXISTING PATHS

Blessings flow best when guided by order. A formed heart without structure is vulnerable. On the other hand, a structure without a formed heart is dangerous because it gives power, resources, or influence to motives that are not surrendered, allowing pride or self-interest to direct what was meant to serve others. Blessing moves without distortion only when a formed heart and the structure to carry it exist together.

So it is with money.

Without boundaries, money can harm a household, fueling impulsive decisions, relational strain, and instability. But it can also vanish without a trace, absorbed into daily consumption, unnoticed spending, and unexamined habits—never gathering into anything that sustains or multiplies. What was meant to become life-giving provision scatters into chaos or disappears into waste.

Systems—budgets, accounts, safeguards—are the riverbanks that prepare for what will eventually flow. They do not restrict blessing; they give it form. They create the capacity to receive, hold, and direct what has been entrusted. With structure in place, money can move intentionally: meeting needs, supporting others, building stability, and extending beyond the present moment.

Without structure, even good provision loses its way.

With structure, even modest provision becomes fruitful.

> *"[B]ut all things should be done decently and in order."*
> 1 CORINTHIANS 14:40

> *"The plans of the diligent lead surely to abundance, but everyone who is hasty comes only to want."*
> PROVERBS 21:5

PRACTICAL APPLICATION: Preparing Financially

These practices are not merely financial strategies to manage what has arrived. They are the means by which what has been received is absorbed, examined, and ordered before it begins to move. Thus, they are *financial disciplines*—Asceticism, Prudence, and a Rule of Life made specific to money. What the previous chapter formed inwardly, this chapter builds outwardly. These are not new principles—they are the same virtues given practical structure, moved from the interior terrain of the heart into the external terrain of life. They are expressions of biblical stewardship, ensuring that what comes does not overwhelm, scatter, or disappear, but is prepared to flow with purpose.

DISCIPLINE 1—PAUSING: *Practice a thirty-day pause rule. No major decisions without prayerful reflection.*

When provision comes, resist the urge to act quickly. Allow what has arrived to settle. This is Prudence's Patience made concrete, the delayed decision given a number and a commitment. It is also the[Rule of Life's first pre-decided rule of safety: no major financial decisions under emotional stress. The thirty-day pause is how both virtues take practical form.

Create intentional time to pray, reflect, and seek wise counsel before making significant decisions. In prayer, ask:

1) What portion belongs to God as first fruits?
2) What portion provides protection and stability?
3) What portion is meant for generosity?
4) What portion contributes to legacy?

These four questions are the Rule of Life's allocation priorities applied in real time—the channels defined before the meltwater begins to move. Decisions are made slowly, often with the guidance of a trusted and qualified professional.

We see this principle in the life of Joseph, who did not react impulsively to abundance during Egypt's years of plenty. Instead, through discernment and preparation, he stored grain over time, creating stability for a future season of need (Genesis 41). What appeared to be delay was wisdom preparing the way for provision to be sustained. Joseph practiced Prudence before the word existed—reading the conditions, resisting urgency, and directing what had been entrusted toward its proper end.

When famine struck, Egypt had food because of Joseph's preparation.

Like snow that settles in the runout zone before it transforms, wise stewardship allows what is given to rest, be examined, and be directed with intention. Blessings require stillness before they can be received, sustained, and multiplied.

DISCIPLINE 2—ORDERING: *Establish order before movement.*

When provision comes, do not allow it to disperse without direction. What is received must be gathered before it is released. This is the Rule of Life's allocation priorities in practice—*ordo amoris* made concrete, each portion assigned to its proper end before movement begins.

One practical way to do this is by creating intentional categories—what some call buckets—for Necessities, Giving, Saving, Investing, Almsgiving, and Enjoyment. These are not literal containers but purposeful distinctions. Each category receives its portion deliberately with clarity about its role.

Giving is not what remains after spending.

Saving is not an afterthought.

Investing is not postponed indefinitely.

Enjoyment is not confused with impulse.

What is received is first assigned, then released.

We also see this pattern in the gathering of manna among the Israelites (Exodus 16). Each household collected what was needed, neither hoarding nor neglecting what had been given. What was received was handled with intention, within boundaries, and according to purpose. Disorder led to spoilage; obedience preserved provision.

In practice, these "buckets" may take the form of accounts, envelopes, or digital budgeting tools that separate what is meant for different purposes. The method matters less than the consistency. This is Prudence's Discernment applied to daily money management—planning before panic, intention before impulse.

Pay attention to what slowly erodes margin.

Small, recurring charges, passive subscriptions, automatic renewals, and unnoticed habits can all disperse resources without direction. Left unexamined, they diminish capacity over time, reducing what could have been directed with purpose.

Like channels carved into the mountain before the meltwater flows, order preserves what has been received. When structure is established in advance, provision is no longer lost to gradual erosion—it is gathered, protected, and prepared to move with purpose.

DISCIPLINE 3—CONSECRATING: *Open a separate "Divine Avalanche Account" to create a place for discernment.*

Before increase is put into motion, it must first be given a place to rest. This is Asceticism's self-ordering made structural—setting apart what has been received before the ordinary demands of daily life absorb it without reflection.

Create a separate space, a "Divine Avalanche Account," to receive what is surplus, unexpected, or newly entrusted. This is not about making the money "special," but about creating room for discernment. When provision flows directly into the same place as daily expenses (groceries, gas, subscriptions, impulse purchases) it is often absorbed without reflection because daily life is immediate and demanding.

To set something apart is to slow it down.

If the name causes you to pause, to pray, or to hesitate before moving what is stored there, then it is serving its purpose.

This principle is deeply rooted in Scripture. Consecration is the practice of setting something apart, assigning it its purpose, and only afterward putting it to use. We see it in the offerings brought to the Temple in the time of Hezekiah. The people brought their first fruits and tithes, gathered into heaps, collected and held before distribution (2 Chronicles 31). What was given to God was not immediately consumed. It was first ordered, accounted for, and stewarded.

Throughout Scripture, this pattern repeats:

❄ The *Sabbath* is consecrated before any work is done (Genesis 2:3).

❄ *First fruits* are offered before the harvest is consumed (Proverbs 3:9–10).

❄ The *Tabernacle* is constructed and anointed before God's presence fills it (Exodus 40).

- The *Temple vessels* are purified before they are used in worship (2 Chronicles 29:16–19).
- The *tithe* is designated as the Lord's portion before the remainder is enjoyed (Leviticus 27:30).
- The *Passover* is established before deliverance is experienced (Exodus 12).
- The *Law* is given before the people enter the Promised Land (Deuteronomy 5–6).

In each case, what is set apart is protected, ordered, and prepared. This is the Rule of Life's pre-decided rules of safety applied to the moment of sudden increase—structure established before the pressure of abundance arrives.

In practice, this means creating a container that is:

- Not linked to a debit card
- Not connected to shopping or daily transactions
- Not used for routine expenses

Its purpose is simple. To receive increase. To hold provision. To allow time for prayer and wise direction. This is Prudence's Patience given a physical form—a place where discernment can happen before decisions are made.

Your operating account is for movement.

Your set-apart account is for discernment.

Like snow resting in the runout zone before it transforms, what is held in stillness is not stagnant; it is being prepared. When abundance comes suddenly, it should not immediately enter circulation. It should first enter consecration.

DISCIPLINE 4—UNBURDENING: *Remove financial burdens that enslave the borrower.*

High-interest debt is not neutral. It is designed to extract, drawing out more than the original obligation by consuming time, attention, margin, and peace. What appears to offer access becomes a form of slow bondage, compounding over time until forward movement feels impossible. This is not merely financial language; it is spiritual insight. Debt, when it grows beyond proportion, narrows freedom, distorts decision-making, and keeps the heart in a posture of reaction rather than discernment.

This is precisely what Asceticism's self-knowledge names: the unnamed burden that retains silent control. What has not been examined cannot be addressed. What has not been brought into the light continues to govern from the shadows.

We see a redemptive picture of release in the story of Elisha and the widow (2 Kings 4:1–7). Faced with overwhelming debt and the threat of losing her sons to creditors, the widow cries out for help. Through obedience and God's provision, her small jar of oil becomes abundance, enough not only to survive, but to pay her debts and live on what remained.

The pattern is clear: first the burden is lifted. Then life is sustained.

Removing oppressive debt is an act of restoration. It reopens what has been constricted. What once leaked away through interest begins to flow again toward provision, stability, and generosity. This is Prudence's ordinary wisdom at work—paying off high-interest debt before anything else, choosing stability over spectacle, and creating margin so that future increase can be carried without strain.

This is not about shame. Many faithful people find themselves caught in systems that profit from urgency and imbalance. The Rule of Life's pre-decided rules of safety exist precisely for this reason—to establish boundaries before pressure arrives—so that debt does not accumulate unchecked while provision leaks away unnoticed.

Like clearing a blocked channel after heavy accumulation, removing these burdens allows what God provides to be held, directed, and released with freedom.

Discipline 5—Honoring: *Set apart first fruits by establishing a rhythm of tithing and generosity.*

Your plan will be personal, shaped by your life, your convictions, and your season.

It is worth acknowledging that tithing has not always been handled well. Many have encountered confusion, pressure, or misuse in how it has been taught. Where something sacred is misunderstood, it becomes distorted. Yet the misuse of a practice does not diminish its purpose. Scripture presents giving not as compulsion but as ordered devotion. Honoring God with what is first is trust made visible. In the early Church, generosity flowed from the heart, not from oversight or enforcement. When approached with clarity and freedom, the fruit of disciplined giving is too significant to ignore.

This is Asceticism's self-ordering applied to generosity, ensuring that giving serves its proper end rather than becoming reactive or entangled with fear.

After returning to the Catholic Church, and after applying the lessons of this book to our own lives, my husband and I chose to set apart our tithe through direct deposit, rather than waiting for the passing of the collection basket. This became a way of honoring first fruits deliberately and consistently. First fruits are not what remain after everything else has been paid. They are what is set apart initially, before anything else is touched.

In Scripture, offerings were brought intentionally and in order, never as an afterthought, and never as a reaction to emotion or circumstance. To give first is to decide in advance that God will be honored before appetite, fear, or impulse has its say. The collection basket can invite generosity, but it can also invite delay. Too often, we give what happens to be available in the moment rather than what we have already resolved in prayer.

This is the Rule of Life's Protection at its most sacred expression—generosity planned in advance, structured before the moment of decision arrives, so that what is given to God cannot be undone by urgency or circumstance.

Modern life offers a way to restore the ancient discipline of first fruits with greater faithfulness. Giving can be arranged ahead of time through scheduled bank transfers, recurring electronic offerings, or automatic withdrawals aligned with income. These practices allow generosity to move first, before spending begins and before money becomes entangled with desire or anxiety. With modern tools—bank bill-pay systems or online platforms such as Tithe.ly, Pushpay, Givelify, Subsplash, or Planning Center—ordered, intentional generosity becomes not only possible but sustainable. This is Prudence's Vision applied to giving—thinking in decades rather than moments, establishing a pattern that outlasts any single season of abundance or scarcity.

In many parishes, this intentional structure is already being encouraged. At Annunciation Catholic Church in Altamonte Springs, Florida, parishioners are invited to distribute their giving thoughtfully through an online giving portal:

- Five percent to the weekly Sunday offertory
- One percent to the diocesan appeal
- Four percent to other charitable works, including care for the poor and special collections

While ten percent is often proposed as a biblical benchmark, the Church does not mandate a fixed percentage. Each person is invited to give prayerfully and proportionately according to their means (CCC 2043).

When giving is ordered in this way, it becomes an act of trust rather than reaction. The offering is released faithfully, consistently, and without fanfare—whether or not we are present, whether or not we feel moved in the moment. It is no less sacred for being planned. In fact, it is more so. What is holy is set apart intentionally.

To arrange first fruits in advance is to say with one's life: God is first, not the leftover.

It frees the heart from negotiation and trains the soul in surrender. The collection basket may still pass, but the gift has already been given. In that ordered faithfulness, generosity becomes a steady rhythm, anchoring abundance to gratitude and blessing to obedience.

Planned generosity transforms giving from a momentary emotion into intentional worship.

DISCIPLINE 6—RESERVING: *Build an emergency fund and protect it.*

This has been the area of greatest struggle for our family. Every time we establish a reserve, an unexpected need draws it back down. It brings to mind a lesson my father taught me long ago: never let the gas tank fall below a quarter full, because you never know when an accident or delay on the road will leave you stranded. Financial margin serves the same purpose. But here is the honest question: why is it so easy to follow the gas tank rule and so difficult to follow the emergency fund rule?

The answer may be simpler than we think. The gas tank is already built into the car. It is the container. You never have to decide to save the gas separately. The structure does it for you and warns you when you get to the quarter-full line. The emergency fund requires intentional separation from your checking account—and life gives no warning light before the need arises. This is Asceticism's self-knowledge applied to reserves: until we name the pattern that keeps drawing the fund back down, we cannot address what governs it.

This is also where the Rule of Life's Protection becomes essential: it holds what has been gathered before pressure can disperse it. But a pre-decided rule—save consistently, automatically, and do not touch it—removes the decision from the moment of pressure.

Scripture commends exactly this. Wisdom stores what is needed without clinging to it. A reserve is discernment about the world God created, where seasons change and interruptions come. Saving honors the truth that life moves in seasons. Scripture further invites us to recognize times of gathering and times of release, without promising that abundance will be uninterrupted. However, God "is able to provide you with every blessing in abundance, so that by always having enough of everything, you may share abundantly in every good work" (2 Corinthians 9:8). Reserves do not isolate us from dependence on God. They steady us within it. A reserve allows us to meet lean seasons without panic or compromise. This is Prudence's Discernment made practical—choosing stability over spectacle, building margin before abundance arrives so that future increase can be carried without strain. Like the deep base layers of the snowpack that never release in the avalanche but hold the mountain steady and feed the groundwater slowly over time, a reserve is not what moves dramatically—it is what makes movement possible without collapse.

Discipline 7—Committing: *Render unto government authorities what belongs to them.*

Sudden increase brings obligations as well as opportunity. Taxes are not a punishment; they are a reality of stewardship in the world as it is. Scripture is direct: "Give therefore to the emperor the things that are the emperor's." (Matthew 22:21; Mark 12:17; Luke 20:25). When abundance arrives, wisdom pauses to ask what is owed before deciding what is enjoyed, given, or invested.

This is Prudence's Counsel made concrete, normalizing professional advice before pressure arrives.

Consulting a qualified advisor before the weight of sudden increase prevents bad decisions that cannot be undone.

A licensed CPA or tax professional can help you calculate tax responsibilities accurately and design boundaries—spending limits, accountability check-ins, emergency thresholds—the kinds of pre-decided rules you will be grateful for later, even if they feel restrictive now. This is the Rule of Life's Protection applied to tax obligation: structure established in advance so that what is owed to governing authorities does not arrive as a surprise that destabilizes what remains.

Understanding tax responsibility ahead of time preserves peace and frees the heart to steward the remainder with confidence and gratitude. Preparation here is not distrust in God. It is respect for the weight of what he has entrusted.

Meeting early with a qualified advisor allows clarity to replace anxiety. It prevents surprise, protects generosity, and ensures that what is meant to bless does not later burden the soul with fear or regret.

In the runout zone, not everything that arrives is yours to keep. Some of what the avalanche carries belongs to others. Wisdom sorts what is owed before directing what remains.

DISCIPLINE 8—PLANTING: *Invest wisely so that provision is not immediately consumed.*

Many people who struggle with structuring their income have never been taught to think this way. For them, money exists only to be spent or stretched—not organized or multiplied. Ask someone how they structure their income and the answer will reveal their posture toward money more honestly than any direct question could.

This is Asceticism's Self-direction at work. It trains the imagination away from consumption and toward stewardship, beginning to ask not only what money could buy but what it could sustain, whom it could bless, and what it could build long after the original provision is gone.

Structured investment gradually reshapes legacy. It teaches the next generation that provision can be stored, protected, and positioned so that it is not immediately consumed. Like the lessons embedded in the game of Monopoly, where owning assets generates income even when you are not actively playing, investment teaches that provision can work on your behalf while you sleep. Investing wisely frees families from constant dependence on active labor alone.

This is Prudence's Vision made practical—thinking in decades rather than moments, establishing a pattern of growth that outlasts any single season of abundance.

Scripture consistently commends this posture. In the Parable of the Talents, Jesus praises the servants who invested what they were given so that it produced more in his absence (Matthew 25:14–30). While this parable can be applied to making disciples, Jesus is teaching most immediately that God entrusts gifts, opportunities, and resources to us, and he expects faithful stewardship rather than fearful inaction. Proverbs also commends diligence that yields enduring return rather than momentary consumption (Proverbs 13:11) and affirms that wise planning leads to sustainable increase: "The plans of the diligent lead surely to abundance" (Proverbs 21:5). Ecclesiastes encourages diversification so that provision continues through uncertain seasons (Ecclesiastes 11:2).

In our time, structured investment may take the form of index funds, real estate, or purposeful business ventures, pursued prayerfully and with wise counsel. This is the Rule of Life's Order applied to growth: the portion designated for investment decided in advance, before abundance arrives and before desire has its say.

Jesus warned against anxious worry about tomorrow, not against wise preparation for it.

The distinction is always the interior posture… whether provision is driven by fear or by faith. Passive income is foresight. It is provision positioned to accumulate over time so that families, communities, and future generations are not left vulnerable when age, illness, job loss, or changing circumstances reduce the ability to earn through labor alone. Like rivers fed by meltwater that carve their own channels over time, wise investment does not merely carry provision. It shapes the terrain through which future blessing will flow.

DISCIPLINE 9—HARVESTING: *Support ministries, charities, or scholarships.*

You might ask: "Aren't tithing and almsgiving enough?" Jesus honored the tithe and pointed beyond it. He praised sacrificial giving, spontaneous mercy, and care for the poor as the fruit of obedience, not its replacement. The tithe flows *toward* God. Generosity flows *outward from* what God has given.

In the early Church, believers continued regular giving while also responding freely to needs as they arose (Acts 2:44–45; 2 Corinthians 9:6–8). The reward for giving generously above and beyond the tithe was: "You will be enriched in every way for your great generosity" (2 Corinthians 9:11).

Both express different dimensions of love rightly ordered:

Tithing is an act of love through *obedience,* placing God first in trust and reverence.

Generosity is an act of love through *overflow*, extending what has been received toward others.

Neither replaces the other. Together they ensure that abundance flows without distortion.

This is Asceticism's Self-direction applied to giving. It is the imagination trained to ask not only what money could buy but whom it could bless and what it could build long after the original gift is given.

In Scripture, giving was ordered. Offerings were set apart deliberately and provision was directed with intention. When giving is left to the moment, it is often shaped by urgency, emotion, or the expectations of others. Prayerful discernment in advance roots giving in conviction. This is Prudence's Vision at work—thinking in decades, understanding that a scholarship funded today or a ministry supported consistently reshapes lives and communities across generations the giver will never see.

A giving plan does not close the heart to unexpected opportunities. It is the Rule of Life's Order applied to generosity: primary commitments established in advance, leaving you free to give beyond them without confusion or strain. Hidden acts of mercy, scholarships, and ministry support all find their place naturally within a plan that has already made room for them.

A giving plan transforms generosity from scattered moments into a steady current, one that reflects calling, sustains joy, and honors God with clarity and purpose. When generosity is given a plan, compassion has a clear channel long before the moment of need arrives.

PREPARE RELATIONALLY:

SET BOUNDARIES BEFORE PRESSURE COMES

Money often changes relationships. Sudden wealth attracts attention, not all of it holy. Some may expect handouts; others may become resentful and distance themselves. Still others may begin to relate to you through your resources instead of your heart.

Eventually, the meltwater will move into directed channels of blessing toward the valley, but not before boundaries are set.

Earlier, God taught us to recognize the doors he opens. Preparation now teaches us that faithful stewardship also requires knowing which doors to close. Every door God opens invites life; every door he closes protects it. As blessing begins to move, wisdom is no longer found only in what we welcome, but also in what we refuse to let enter.

Relational boundaries protect love by protecting the conditions in which love can flourish. They do this not by opening another door, but by wisely *closing one.* Every healthy boundary says no to something destructive so that it can continue to say yes to something life-giving.

> *"Do not be one of those who give pledges, who become surety for debts. If you have nothing with which to pay, why should your bed be taken from under you?"*
> PROVERBS 22:26–27

Boundaries are not the opposite of love; they are one of its expressions. Jesus loved freely, yet he never allowed urgency, expectation, or manipulation to dictate his mission. He regularly withdrew to pray (Luke 5:16), declined demands that conflicted with the Father's will (Mark 1:35–38), and always gave what people truly needed rather than merely what they desired. Healthy boundaries allow us to do the same.

> *"Iron sharpens iron, and one person sharpens the wits of another."*
> PROVERBS 27:17

> *"If it is possible, so far as it depends on you, live peaceably with all."*
> ROMANS 12:18

They free us to give joyfully instead of resentfully, wisely instead of reactively, and faithfully instead of fearfully.

> *"Where there is no guidance, a nation falls, but in an abundance of counselors there is safety."*
> PROVERBS 11:14

PRACTICAL APPLICATION: Preparing Relationally

Just as channels are formed as the snow melts, *relational boundaries* must be established before increase so when requests come, your response is guided rather than reactive. The Avalanche Examen revealed what lives beneath the surface in stillness. The three mental disciplines gave structure to your thinking in motion. Relational boundaries now become the guardrails that protect that movement—because what is not properly contained will eventually be tested under increase. When blessing comes, relationships will press against the edges of your heart, and your boundaries should already be firmly in place.

BOUNDARY 1: CLOSE THE DOOR ON RESPONDING IN THE MOMENT. *Decide in advance how you will respond to requests.*

Money has a way of drawing petitions toward us. Some are sincere, some urgent, some manipulative, and some simply unprepared. When abundance arrives suddenly, requests often follow just as quickly. Boundaries are not created in the moment they are needed; they are formed long before they are tested. The pressure to give makes it nearly impossible to create.

This is Asceticism's self-knowledge applied to relationship—naming the pattern before pressure arrives so it no longer governs unconsciously. And it is the Rule of Life's Protection made relational: a pre-decided response that removes the need to deliberate when guilt, urgency, or expectation is pressing against the heart.

Write a simple boundary line you can return to when emotions or pressure threaten to override your judgment. For example: "We do not have the financial reserves to respond to individual requests at this time." Having language prepared protects you from decisions driven by guilt, urgency, or pressure. A heart without boundaries soon becomes resentful. A heart with wise boundaries remains free to give gladly, prayerfully, and without fear in the future.

Deciding beforehand how you will respond to family, friends, or strangers allows generosity to remain clear of guilt because it is rooted in conviction rather than emotion. It guards relationships from becoming transactional and prevents giving from being shaped by expectation rather than calling.

Healthy boundaries ask important questions ahead of time:

1) What am I called to give freely?
2) What requires prayer and counsel?
3) What is beyond my responsibility, even if it feels uncomfortable to say no?

When boundaries are established early, and expectations are clear, responses can be given calmly and consistently, especially when conflict arises. Generosity, then, becomes an act of obedience rather than reaction, and relationships are preserved rather than strained.

BOUNDARY 2: CLOSE THE DOOR ON MISTAKING PROXIMITY FOR CALLING. *Acknowledge that not every request that reaches you is yours to answer.*

Often, requests and petitions come from those closest to you: family members, longtime friends, people whose needs feel urgent simply because you love them. Others come from strangers, organizations, or causes that arrive with compelling stories and genuine needs. Both can be worthy. Neither is automatically your responsibility.

Proximity is not the same as calling. The fact that someone is near does not mean their need has been assigned to you. And the fact that someone is unknown does not disqualify their need from your generosity. What discerns between the two is not closeness but covenant—the commitments, convictions, and callings God has already established in your life.

Family requests carry a particular weight because they arrive wrapped in history, love, and shared identity. Saying no can feel like rejection. Saying yes without discernment can slowly shift a relationship from covenantal to transactional, where the one with resources becomes the one from whom resources are expected. Wisdom here requires both tenderness and clarity. It honors the relationship without surrendering discernment to it.

Requests from strangers, whether they are individuals, organizations, or causes, require a different kind of wisdom. Without an existing relationship, there is no natural accountability, no shared history, and no easy way to discern whether giving serves or enables. This is where your giving plan, already established, does its work. When commitments are decided in advance, responses to unfamiliar requests can be calm rather than reactive, rooted in calling rather than guilt.

In both cases, the same question applies: Is this mine to carry? Not every need is a personal assignment. Discernment is the practice of giving where God has called, not where the pressure has surfaced. This is

Prudence applied to relationship—reading the terrain before stepping, discerning what is stable, and resisting the pressure of proximity when divine calling points elsewhere.

BOUNDARY 3: CLOSE THE DOOR ON ASSUMPTIONS.

Keep family conversations honest and consistent.

Discernment about who is asking you to give is only half the work. The other half is what happens inside the immediate family itself… the conversations that either build shared understanding or allow assumptions to harden into expectation.

Talk openly about how money will, and will not, be used. Clarity prevents assumptions, reduces entitlement, and protects relationships from quiet resentment. Money matters left unspoken often become misunderstood. Expectations form in silence, and what is unexpressed can slowly erode trust. Honest conversation brings what is hidden into the light, allowing relationships to remain rooted in truth rather than assumption. This kind of clarity may seem harsh, but it is protective. It ensures that generosity is received as a gift, not assumed as an obligation, and that love is not confused with access.

When families speak plainly and early, they create shared understanding. Boundaries become known, expectations become realistic, and unity is preserved even as circumstances change. Clarity prevents resentment, and honesty protects trust. Healthy relationships rarely collapse from a single difficult conversation; they erode through many conversations that never happened.

BOUNDARY 4: CLOSE THE DOOR ON CONFUSING COMPASSION WITH OBLIGATION. *Give because God leads you, not because pressure compels you.*

You may feel moved to help, but you are not called to be everyone's provider. Compassion is a gift; obligation, when assumed without discernment, can become a burden that distorts both giving and relationship. Not every need is yours to meet. Some are invitations to pray, to guide, or simply to walk alongside. Wisdom learns to discern the difference.

At times, the most loving response is not immediate provision, but honest presence: "I can't do that, but I will pray with you and help you think through your options." This kind of response redirects love toward what it can actually reach. It honors both the dignity of the other person and the boundaries of your own calling.

When compassion is separated from obligation, generosity remains free. It is no longer driven by guilt or pressure, but guided by truth, prayer, and responsibility. In this way, love is purified—freed to give as God gives.

BOUNDARY 5: CLOSE THE DOOR ON ALLOWING WEALTH TO REDEFINE YOUR IDENTITY. *Maintain humility as wealth grows.*

Wealth does not only test the soul; it tests relationships. As resources increase, dynamics shift how others perceive us, how freely people speak to us, and how willing we remain to listen. As we will examine later, King Solomon's kingdom paid the price (1 Kings 11-12). His son, Rehoboam, inherited immense wealth and power but lacked humility, seeking counsel among his peers instead of the elders. His arrogance led him to burden the people and reject wisdom, placing him in ongoing conflict with Jeroboam, to whom the Lord had given ten of the twelve tribes. The lesson is clear:

What Rehoboam had not been formed to carry, he could not sustain.

The deeper temptation is not always immediate pride, but gradual self-sufficiency: a slow drift from dependence on God and community to confidence in provision itself. This is why Prudence is relational wisdom as much as financial wisdom; it is the long view that keeps wealth in its proper place as seasons change.

Scripture consistently warns that abundance can dull discernment if humility is not actively preserved. Wealth is not dangerous because it exists, but because it can subtly draw trust away from God and toward security, influence, or independence. When that shift occurs, relationships are often the first to suffer.

Relational humility requires intentional remembrance. It means recognizing that every increase is received, not earned in isolation. It means remaining teachable, staying connected to people who knew you before the increase, and continuing to seek counsel even when you no longer need it financially. Humility keeps wealth in its proper place as a tool, not an identity. Faith remains relational when gratitude is practiced openly, generosity is extended without display, and counsel is welcomed consistently. Balanced wealth does not announce itself. It is marked by constancy, restraint, and steady confidence rather than display or control.

As provision grows, humility protects relationships. It keeps conversations honest, authority gentle, and influence accountable. In this way, increase becomes a means of service rather than self-protection, and blessing remains aligned with its true purpose, anchoring us more deeply in love, trust, and responsibility.

BOUNDARY 6: CLOSE THE DOOR ON ISOLATED DECISION-MAKING. *Seek wise counsel.*

Invite a trusted mentor, advisor, or spiritual leader who can lovingly say, "This choice aligns" or "This feels like pressure, not purpose."

Increase has a way of isolating. As resources grow, fewer people feel free to speak honestly, and fewer questions are asked. Accountability protects against this slow movement away from purpose. Staying connected to mentors, church leadership, or trusted counsel ensures that decisions are tested, not merely justified.

> *"As for those who in the present age are rich, command them not to be haughty…. They are to do good, to be rich in good works, generous, and ready to share…."*
> 1 TIMOTHY 6:17–18

Biblical accountability is about shared wisdom, mutual encouragement, and growth in holiness. Scripture reminds us that "in an abundance of counselors there is safety" (Proverbs 11:14). Wise counsel offers perspective when emotion clouds judgment, and grounding when success tempts us to be self-reliant. This is the Rule of Life's Vigilance applied to relationship—the regular review that prevents drift before it becomes collapse.

True accountability is chosen, not imposed. It means inviting a small circle of trusted voices who can ask difficult questions, challenge assumptions, and reflect both blind spots and growth with clarity and grace. I will be honest. This is the boundary I have found hardest to maintain. But I have never regretted it. In doing so, humility is preserved, faith remains active, and stewardship stays aligned with its deeper purpose.

BOUNDARY 7: CLOSE THE DOOR ON FUNDING FAMILY OUT OF ORDER. *Fund family after giving and saving are established.*

Notice where this step falls: after saving in buckets, after ordering our giving and generosity, after seeking wise counsel. That placement is not an accident of arrangement. It is the argument.

Chapter 6 asked you to prepare the heart spiritually. This is where that formation takes visible shape—or fails to.

> *"But strive first for the kingdom of God and his righteousness, and all these things will be given to you as well."*
> MATTHEW 6:33

The verse sits at the heart of the Sermon on the Mount, inside Jesus' teaching on worry, provision, and trust (Matthew 6:25–34). It is not a promise offered from a distance. In verse 31 he names the anxieties directly:

- ❄ What will we eat?
- ❄ What will we drink?
- ❄ What will be wear?

Earlier he points to the birds of the air and the lilies of the field, showing that God is attentive to real, material needs. Jesus is not spiritualizing hunger or dismissing responsibility; he is restoring the right order of our loves. That is *ordo amoris* applied to the household budget. That sequence can be difficult to accept, especially for those of us whose first instinct is to provide immediately and generously for our children. I say this as someone still learning it. One of the final frontiers in our own household has been becoming more intentional about both how quickly we respond and how much we spend on our sons. What often feels like love can drift into excess, and what begins as generosity can drift into entitlement without our realizing it. Excess, given without formation, can corrupt what it was meant to nourish. Scripture cautions against indulgence without formation, reminding us that what is given too freely, without wisdom or discipline, can ultimately harm the very child we are trying to bless (Proverbs 13:24). In our culture of expectation, it is easy to measure care through performance, comparison, and achievement—to equate doing more and providing more with loving more. But care without intention can blur the line between what truly forms a child and what merely satisfies the momentary needs.

When giving is rightly ordered, how much we give becomes a question of what is left to give after giving and saving have been arranged. Giving first acknowledges

God as the source. Saving next provides stability and protection. Only then does investment in family move from urgency to wisdom. When family needs are funded before giving and saving are established, provision often becomes reactive… driven by fear, guilt, or immediacy. This is where predatory lenders find their opening, when provision is disordered and urgency drives decisions. But when generosity and stability are secured first, investing in family becomes thoughtful rather than anxious. Decisions about education, health, and opportunity are made purposefully and clearly, not hastily and haphazardly.

This order of giving strengthens care for family. It ensures that support is sustainable, that resources are not exhausted prematurely, and that provision does not come at the expense of peace or obedience. In this way, family investment becomes part of legacy rather than a drain on it, rooted in faith, reinforced by stability, and guided by discernment.

BOUNDARY 8: CLOSE THE DOOR ON ENABLING DESTRUCTIVE PATTERNS IN OTHERS. *Give God the space to do what only he can do.*

"Hold on… so now we have to worry about enabling others?" Yes! People are watching—our children most of all—and they are learning, often not through instruction but through unspoken observation. While you are not responsible for their growth (their growth is God's work, not yours), much of what is absorbed is not conscious imitation, but unconscious formation. While we are not called to fix others, the Apostle Paul reminds us that we are called to imitate Christ.

> *"Be imitators of me, as I am of Christ."*
> 1 CORINTHIANS 11:1

Yet, Scripture distinguishes between burdens (which we help carry) and loads (which belong to the individual).

> *"For all must carry their own loads."*
> GALATIANS 6:5

> *"Anyone unwilling to work should not eat."*
> 2 THESSALONIANS 3:10

> *"Laziness brings on deep sleep; an idle person will suffer hunger."*
> PROVERBS 19:15

The way we handle money, respond to requests, and set boundaries teaches others what is normal, permissible, and sustainable.

When generosity lacks discernment, it can unintentionally reinforce dependency rather than maturity.

Enabling removes or reduces the natural consequences of another person's unhealthy or irresponsible behavior in ways that allow those patterns to continue. And while we are not accountable for whether someone grows, we are being entrusted with faithfulness in how we live and give, that others might see Christ in us. Jesus offers a sobering reminder of our influence:

> *"If any of you put a stumbling block before one of these little ones who believe in me, it would be better for you if a great millstone were fastened around your neck and you were drowned in the depth of the sea."*
>
> MATTHEW 18:6

Little ones not only refer to children, but anyone who has an innocent faith in Christ (or a vulnerable person). To lead them into confusion, dependency, or harm, however unintentionally, is something Scripture treats with great seriousness. This verse appears in Jesus' discourse on humility and the kingdom of heaven, where he calls his followers to become like little children. The warning in Matthew 18:6 (also echoed in Mark 9:42 and Luke 17:2) stresses that harming such vulnerable individuals is an offense against God himself, incurring severe judgment.

How, then, did Jesus love without enabling? He consistently gave people what they truly needed, not always what they immediately wanted. He fed the hungry, but he did not continue multiplying bread every day after they sought him only for food (John 6). He healed many, but he also told people, "Go and sin no more" (John 8:11). He restored Peter, but first required him to confront his failure: "Do you love me?" (John 21:15–19). He welcomed the rich young ruler yet refused to lower the cost of discipleship (Mark 10:17–22). Christ's compassion never bypassed truth, responsibility, or transformation. Neither should ours.

In view of this, discernment thus becomes an act of love. It protects not only what we give, but how it is received. True generosity does not merely relieve the moment; it seeks the other person's good. It strengthens character, encourages maturity, and points the heart toward Christ rather than toward dependence on us.

CLOSING REFLECTION

Readiness is not a lack of faith or fear of the unknown. It is faith with a backbone. The steps in this chapter—buckets, first fruits, guardrails, boundaries, counsel, conversations—are not about trying to control what God will do next. They are about honoring what he has already done and treating blessing like something sacred instead of something casual.

Abundance does not only test our money habits; it tests our peace. It tests our relationships. It tests our humility. And if we are not careful, what was meant to nourish can overwhelm. Just as a river requires banks to keep it from becoming a flood, generosity requires boundaries to remain life-giving. Every door we wisely close—to pressure, manipulation, unhealthy obligation, and enabling—protects the channels through which God's blessing is meant to flow. Boundaries do not restrict love; they preserve it.

Everything you have prayed through in this chapter—from opening a separate "Divine Avalanche" account to paying off predatory debt, setting boundaries, and having difficult conversations—is not about controlling the future. It is about honoring God with the present. Taken together, these practices form a declaration that your heart belongs to God first and that money is to be stewarded not possessed.

None of this guarantees that the divine avalanche will come in the way you imagine.

It does something better.

It shapes you into the kind of person who can carry weight without being crushed by it—and the kind of steward who can receive much or little and remain the same beloved child of God in either case. For God is often more concerned with preparing the steward than with delivering the blessing.

You have not just made a plan; you have made space. Space for peace instead of panic. Space for wisdom instead of impulse. Space for generosity protected by healthy boundaries. Space for rivers instead of floods.

For additional reflection, Scripture provides us with several notable examples of what this readiness looks like:

- *Joseph* prepared faithfully, and when abundance arrived, he sustained nations rather than hoarding provision for himself (Genesis 41–47).
- *Ruth* received favor through humility and obedience, and her unwavering faithfulness grew into a legacy far beyond her lifetime (Ruth 1–4).
- *The disciples* waited in prayer and obedience, and when the Spirit was poured out, the Church was born and multiplied (Acts 1–2).

When the divine avalanche comes, however it comes and whenever it comes, may it find you anchored, ordered, and available, ready not only to receive but to pour out. In the end, preparation is worship.

Reader's Prayer: Preparation as Worship

Lord, if You choose to send abundance,
I will be ready to honor You with it.
If You choose to move slowly,
I will still be faithful.
Whether the snow gathers or the rivers run low,
my trust is not in the avalanche,
but in the One
who commands the mountain, the snow, and the seasons. We honor You as our Source, our Provider, and our Shepherd.
Forgive us for the ways we have treated money as a measure of safety, control, or worth.
Forgive us for the times we have reacted in fear,
or avoided wisdom because it felt overwhelming or humiliating.
Teach us to prepare—not as people trying to engineer blessing, but as children learning to steward what belongs to You.
Form in us financial order that reflects Your peace.
Give us the humility to build the banks before the river runs: to budget with honesty, to separate what is holy from what is common, to set aside first fruits without delay, and to create guardrails that protect our household from impulse and instability.
Give us courage to face what needs repair—debt, leakage, disorder—and the patience to build stability layer by layer.
Make us faithful with little, so we can be trusted with more.
Form in us relational wisdom that reflects Your love.
Teach us boundaries that do not harden compassion, but guard it, so we can say yes freely, no faithfully, and wait without guilt.
Protect our marriages, our children, our friendships, and our communities from comparison, entitlement, manipulation, and resentment.

Keep us teachable.
Keep us connected to wise counsel.
Keep us from isolation and pride.
Let our generosity be guided by calling, not pressure.
Form in us generational clarity that reflects Your covenant.
Help us think beyond ourselves.
Give us the discipline to plan, to write, to document, and to direct what You entrust, so our provision does not become a source of confusion for those we love.
Teach us to leave not only resources, but wisdom;
not only inheritance, but instruction;
not only assets, but a living testimony of trust. Let our legacy carry faith, generosity, stability, and purpose into the lives of children and grandchildren we may never fully see.
Lord, we place our preparation into Your hands.
Bless the quiet steps—the phone call, the budget, the conversation, the account, the boundary, the will.
Let each one be a "yes" to Your order,
a "yes" to Your peace,
and a "yes" to the future You are shaping through us.
If You choose to send abundance, let it find us ready and humble.
If You choose to withhold for a season, let us remain faithful and grateful.
Either way, make our lives a river—not a flood and not a dam—so that what You give becomes life to others and brings glory to Your name.
We worship You with our planning.
We worship You with our restraint.
We worship You with our generosity.
We worship You with our obedience.
In Jesus' name,
Amen.

Johnny Beloved and Preparation

Preparation is invisible. It is the snowpack beneath the surface. It is what happens before deployment—before checks are written, before capital is allocated, before generosity is announced. Snow does not become dangerous because it exists. It becomes dangerous when the layers beneath it are never examined.

Preparation is covenantal obedience in practical form. Israel gathered manna faithfully for forty years before entering the Promised Land. In most cases, formation precedes inheritance.

Johnny Beloved's case is different. The money has already arrived. The avalanche has already fallen. He must now prepare in response to what has been released. Even so, the principle remains the same: preparation determines whether access multiplies or access destabilizes, whether the inheritance enters a prayerful pause or is dispersed immediately and impulsively. The avalanche has come either way. Now his preparation determines whether it buries him… or builds a river.

But Scripture adds a deeper layer: preparedness is not only technical. It is spiritual. The Certain Poor Widow did not give because she had surplus; she gave because she trusted God in lack. Abraham did not obey because he understood outcomes; he obeyed because he was open and teachable. Their posture was not control; it was surrender.

So, before Johnny builds spreadsheets, he must answer a more subtle question: Will he surrender the blessing back to the Giver before he attempts to steward it?

Johnny Beloved has $7.4 million. Now we watch him prepare in response to the inheritance, or fail to.

UNFORMED JOHNNY

Johnny tells himself he will "figure it out."

He watches YouTube finance videos.

He listens to podcasts on 2x speed.

He scrolls investment threads late at night.

Information feels like preparation, but information is not structure. More importantly, information is not surrender.

Johnny does not pause to pray. He does not ask what God desires. He does not place the inheritance back on the altar of trust. Instead, he feels responsible to make the money prove something.

He treats the inheritance as a problem to solve rather than a trust to surrender. As a result, he begins moving before building. He opens accounts impulsively. He moves chunks of money without understanding tax consequences. He says yes to a private placement before reviewing lock-up terms. He hires an advisor but chooses one who flatters him.

He avoids hard conversations about:

❄ Risk tolerance

❄ Long-term allocation

- ❄ Liquidity strategy
- ❄ Estate planning
- ❄ Philanthropic structure

He never builds categories. He never separates accounts. He never stops to think. He never decides what belongs to God, what belongs to protection, and what belongs to legacy. Those conversations feel slow, and Johnny feels urgency. He tells himself, "I can't let the money just sit." But what he calls movement is actually exposure.

He deploys:

- ❄ Without a written investment thesis
- ❄ Without a capital preservation strategy
- ❄ Without understanding his own emotional risk triggers
- ❄ Without financial "banks" to guide the flow
- ❄ Without relational boundaries to protect his peace

Preparation feels like delay. So he skips it.

Six months later....

Two investments need more capital.

One startup pivots unexpectedly.

He owes taxes he did not anticipate.

His giving commitments exceed sustainable cash flow.

His capital is not gone, but it is stressed. And so is he. Because unprepared abundance creates fragility.

He has access, but no structure.

He has opportunity, but no boundaries.

He has movement, but no direction.

Now he has exposure. Whatever is disordered will be revealed in motion; what is not structured before release will fracture under it. And the deepest problem is not the deals. It is that Johnny never surrenders his fear, so he tries to outrun it. He never builds the banks, so the water has nowhere safe to go.

FORMED JOHNNY

Johnny does something uncomfortable.

He pauses… not just to be smart, but to become surrendered.

For three months, he does not invest a dollar beyond short-term safe vehicles. He learns something uncomfortable—time is not the enemy of stewardship; urgency often is. He also learns that patience is not inactivity. Preparation is protection.

His first act of preparation is not research but yielding. Johnny prays a simple prayer: "Father, this is yours. I am not the owner. I am the steward. Don't let me build my life on what can be lost."

He names what is underneath the urgency: grief, fear, and the desire to be approved. He places those drives under God's authority before he places a single dollar anywhere else.

He also recognizes another type of pressure: expectations from others because of proximity. Friends begin suggesting investments. Relatives hint at needs. Opportunities arrive wrapped in relationships. Johnny realizes that preparation must also include the courage to say no.

So before he moves money, he builds structure.

He separates the inheritance from his daily accounts.

He creates clear categories: giving, saving, investing, generosity, enjoyment.

He decides what belongs to God first, before anything else is touched.

He establishes a pause: no major decisions without prayer, time, and counsel.

He builds the banks before the river runs.

Then, he studies.

First, he learns that Israel's tithing system supported worship, priests, widows, foreigners, and the poor.

Then he reads about asset allocation, inflation exposure, and tax drag. He explores donor-advised funds and builds a written financial philosophy.

He connects regularly with his main fiduciary—not someone impressed by him, but someone willing to challenge him.

He asks:

- What percentage must be preserved?
- What percentage can be risked?
- What is the long-term vision?
- What would constitute "enough"?

To ensure blessing flows through him rather than terminating in him, he builds tiers of capital:

- Preservation capital (Treasury bills, high-grade bonds, insured savings)
- Growth capital (index funds, diversified equities, real estate, business ownership)
- Kingdom/generosity capital (missions, donor-advised funds, tithing)
- Experimental capital (startups, new ventures, creative projects)

He does not move from emotion. He builds policies that contain the risks of exciting ideas.

Preparation humbles him. It reveals what he does not know. Humility stabilizes him.

He studies his father's old documents, noticing patterns, like:

- ❄ Slow acquisition
- ❄ Low leverage
- ❄ Long investment holds

He recognizes a pattern: his father's wealth was not built by one violent avalanche. It was built by disciplined accumulation that allowed several divine avalanche moments to be absorbed.

Johnny builds snowpack, layer by layer:

- ❄ Financial literacy
- ❄ Emotional awareness
- ❄ Strategic patience
- ❄ Governance structures
- ❄ Relational boundaries
- ❄ Generational clarity

He begins to name what he has been gripping.

He releases the need to prove that the inheritance was deserved, that he is worthy of what his father built. He releases the fear that if he does not move quickly, the money will somehow slip away or lose its power. He releases the identity he had already begun constructing around the number on the screen. He releases the approval of the people calling, the cousin with the restaurant concept, the college roommate with the startup, the crypto consultant who sent the pitch deck before Johnny had even responded to the text.

None of these are financial decisions. They are acts of surrender. Like the poor widow, he releases what he cannot afford to lose—not the coins themselves, but the security he had placed in them. Like Abraham, he obeys before outcomes are visible, not because he understands what God will do with the inheritance but because he has decided that God, not the inheritance, will determine who he is.

When opportunity knocks now, he does not react.

He evaluates and prepares his next steps.

He has learned that not every opportunity is an assignment and that discernment now governs motion.

Preparation gives him margin, and margin gives him clarity.

Clarity protects capital and financial structure protects peace.

The inheritance no longer defines him. It becomes something he stewards rather than something that explains who he is.

The avalanche has fallen.

The runout zone will hold.

Because Johnny is no longer trying to use the blessing to secure himself. He is letting God secure him… and then stewarding from that security.

He has built the riverbanks.

Now the meltwater can flow.

STAGE IV

Opportunity

The Meltwater Phase

Is This the Right Time to Move?

OPPORTUNITY is when a person's readiness really gets tested. It is discernment meeting the diligence and obedience of the Preparation stage and surrendering it so that it can be transformed into nourishment, sending it on its way down the mountain and along the various chutes of blessings.

We are standing at the *runout zone*. The avalanche has landed. Now the temperature is rising and all that snow you worked so hard to build, melts. But for that meltwater to become a life-giving river instead of runoff, you must have the sagacity and courage to judge well, to understand the complex situations that arise at this level, and to distinguish the subtle details that enable the meltwater to flow down to its final destination: the valley.

You may recall from Chapter 1 on Map to Movement that provision is not the same thing as blessing, that the presence of something is not the same as the benefit of something. Provision may exist but nourishment is absent. Snow that never melts cannot become life. Nourishment occurs only when what is received is metabolized, ordered, and directed. This transformation is not optional; it is the natural result of release. And in order for the meltwater to become a blessing, it must be guided by order.

And here lies the danger: water that is not directed will not wait nor preserve itself. It will become runoff, lost to the ground, absorbed without purpose, or scattered beyond recovery. What had the potential to become a river can be lost in a moment of neglect. The avalanche fell after spiritual and mental preparation. What was built in stillness is now in motion. Opportunity must now be stewarded. However…

The runout zone is the most dangerous position on the mountain.

If the snow did not already bury you, then your next move will determine if you grow from the experience or disappear with the runoff. When flow begins, spiritual risk increases. Momentum can be mistaken for guidance. Urgency can masquerade as calling. And what feels like divine opportunity may simply be movement without direction. For this reason, discernment becomes more critical here than at any other stage of the journey.

Diligence built the snow.

Discernment must now guide the water.

Diligence formed capacity through faithful, consistent obedience.

Surrendered Discernment now determines direction: what to pursue, what to refuse, and where life truly flows.

This is why humility is essential here. Not every movement should be followed. Not every open path leads to life. What appears to be flow may simply be dissipation.

The chapters that follow exist because opportunity is where blessing and danger stand closest together. Here we learn to recognize false flow, to pause when momentum deceives, and to establish the guardrails that turn movement into rivers. Before the water is fully carried forward, the channels must be clear.

8

BUT WAIT… Didn't Jesus Say It's Easier for a Camel to Go Through the Eye of a Needle Than for a Rich Man to Enter the Kingdom of God?

Opportunity is where many hidden assumptions about blessing begin to surface. It is easy to welcome the idea of increase when it is distant or abstract. It is far more unsettling when movement becomes real—when provision, success, or wealth are no longer metaphors but lived possibilities.

At precisely this threshold, Scripture introduces a tension that has troubled believers for centuries. If blessing may flow, if increase may come, if God may indeed release abundance, why does Jesus speak so starkly about wealth? Why does he warn that riches can endanger the soul? Why does he describe the difficulty of a rich man entering the kingdom of God in such arresting imagery?

Before we proceed further into the dynamics of blessing and increase, we must pause here. Opportunity without clarity invites distortion, and few areas of

Christian thought have produced more confusion than the relationship between wealth and salvation.

Jesus first gives the Beatitude (blessing):

> *"Blessed are you who are poor,*
> *for yours is the kingdom of God."*
> LUKE 6:20

Then, he gives the corresponding woe:

> *"But woe to you who are rich,*
> *for you have received your consolation."*
> LUKE 6:24

The Catholic tradition has long made an important distinction in interpreting this warning: wealth itself is not condemned; attachment to wealth is. Material resources can serve God's purposes when they are received as gifts and stewarded with freedom. But when the heart begins to cling to possessions as sources of identity, security, or control, those same resources become spiritually dangerous. As the Catechism of the Catholic Church explains in its reflection on the Beatitudes, the risk lies in making riches our consolation: "The Lord grieves over the rich, because they find their consolation in the abundance of goods" (CCC 2547). This insight echoes St. Augustine's teaching on the ordering of love. In *On Christian Doctrine* (I.4) he writes, "We have wandered far from God, and if we wish to return to our Father's home, this world must be used, not enjoyed, that so the invisible things of God may be clearly seen, being understood by the things that are made—that is, that by means of what is material and temporal we may lay hold upon that which is spiritual and eternal." Augustine makes clear that the problem is not the possession of wealth, but the tendency to rest in created goods as one's consolation rather than in God.

This brings us to one of the most misunderstood sayings of Christ and the subsequent question: "But wait… didn't Jesus say it's easier for a camel to pass through the eye of a needle than for a rich man to enter the kingdom of God?"

Scripture does not give us a single warning about wealth; it gives us a landscape of examples.

I. The Story of the Rich Young Ruler: *Wealth is Not the Barrier (Matthew 19:16–26)*

In the Gospel of Matthew, a young ruler ran to Jesus with sincerity and urgency. He was moral, disciplined, and wealthy. "Teacher, what good deed must I do to have eternal life?" he asked. Jesus affirmed his obedience to the commandments but then pressed deeper. "If you wish to be perfect, go," Jesus said, "sell your possessions, and give the money to the poor, and you will have treasure in heaven; then come, follow me" (Matthew 19:21).

When the young ruler heard this word, he went away grieving because he was very rich.

When Jesus spoke these words, he shocked his disciples:

> *"Again I tell you, it is easier for a camel to go through the eye of a needle than for someone who is rich to enter the kingdom of God."*
> Matthew 19:24

At first glance, it may sound as though Jesus condemned wealth itself. But the story reveals something far more precise. Jesus was addressing a young man whose life was deeply bound to his possessions—to the status, responsibilities, and security they represented. When Jesus invited him to follow, the man walked away in sorrow, not simply because he possessed wealth, but because wealth possessed him. His resources were no longer tools; they had become his master.

Jesus was exposing misplaced trust. Money was never his target.

Wealth becomes spiritually dangerous when it fuses with the structures of the self, when resources cease to function merely as instruments and instead become carriers of identity. Money can gradually assume roles it was never meant to bear. It can become proof of worth, an anchor of selfhood, a signal of status, a measure of success, even a substitute for security itself. In such conditions, wealth is no longer something a person simply possesses, but something by which the person feels defined.

This is the hidden instability of abundance.

When identity attaches to provision, any threat to wealth becomes a threat to the self.

Loss feels like diminishment. Uncertainty becomes existential. Fear intensifies because the self has become entangled with what can fluctuate, not because resources are scarce.

In this way, wealth often produces fragility where we expected stability. Jesus' invitation to the young ruler reached deeper than economics; it was structural. He was asking for something deeper than the surrender of possessions: the release of an attachment by which wealth had become inseparable from identity. The ruler's sorrow arose from the weight of what money had come to represent.

Notice the disciples' reaction. They were stunned:

> *"Then who can be saved?"*
> Matthew 19:25

Jesus replied with hope:

> *"For mortals it is impossible, but for God all things are possible."*
> Matthew 19:26

In other words, God can free the heart that wealth has entangled. The question is not, "Do you have resources?" The question is, "Do resources have you?" Wealth can convince us that we do not need God. It can promise security, identity, status, and control… and then demand our devotion in return. Sudden wealth, especially, can expose attachments we did not realize were there. It reveals where we look for safety, meaning, and power. Before God entrusts abundance, he often heals the heart, forming within it the capacity to *receive* without being *ruled.*

Lesson #1

Wealth itself is not the barrier. The barrier is attachment.

When Jesus asked for surrender, the man chose security over discipleship. Wealth became an idol, a tool turned inward. This matters because Jesus proclaimed that the kingdom of God was at hand—not only as a distant future hope, but as a present reality breaking into ordinary life. The kingdom is God's reign expressed in our decisions, relationships, resources, and priorities. Avalanche theology assumes this truth: God works here and now, in the world where snow accumulates, where rivers of meltwater nourish life, and where valleys receive.

Heaven remains our final reward, but the kingdom does not begin only when we die. It begins wherever Christ is Lord—including how we steward money, respond to blessing, and shape what will outlive us. Our formation today prepares us not only for eternity, but also for wise and faithful influence on the earth God has entrusted to us.

This is why formation matters so deeply. While there are those who claim that the Bible is just a book of fables, the Church has always recognized that God reveals truth through narrative precisely because stories carry truth beyond our defensive walls.

Just as there are lessons in wealth to be gleaned from the rich young ruler in the Gospel of Matthew, other stories invite us to listen, reflect, and allow the Holy Spirit to search our hearts:

II. ACHAN: *When Wealth Is Hidden Instead of Surrendered (Joshua 7)*

After Jericho fell to Joshua and the Israelite army, the city was devoted to the Lord, and the sacred portion of the spoils—the gold, silver, bronze, and iron—was to be placed in the treasury of the Lord. But Achan, from the tribe of Judah, secretly kept a beautiful mantle from Shinar, two hundred shekels of silver, and a bar of gold, hiding them beneath his tent.

The result was devastating.

Israel was defeated at Ai, and the hidden sin affected the whole camp until God revealed Achan and everything connected to his disobedience. He, along with all that he possessed and the stolen items, was brought to the Valley of Achor, where they were stoned, and then burned, as a solemn warning to Israel.

Lesson #2

Wealth withheld harms more than the one who hides it.

The deeper issue is not the silver or the cloak; it is the heart that could not release them. Achan's story and the rich young ruler share the same truth: possessions become dangerous only when they possess us. God does not expose what we hide in order to shame us but to set us free. The same God who warned Israel in the Valley of Achor is the God Jesus revealed when he said, "What is impossible for mortals is possible for God" (Luke 18:27). What destroys when hidden can become redeemed when surrendered.

III. THE WIDOW OF ZAREPHATH: *Trust That Unlocks Provision (1 Kings 17)*

During a drought that led to widespread famine, the prophet Elijah encountered a widow in the Phoenician territory of Zarephath, ten miles south of Sidon, on the coast of the Mediterranean Sea. She was preparing her last bread from meal and oil for herself and her son before death. Elijah asked her to feed him first—an impossible request. She obeyed. Her jar of flour did not run dry, and her oil did not fail.

Lesson #3

God's provision follows trust, not surplus.

What unlocked provision for the widow was not abundance; it was willingness. She gave from emptiness, not overflow, and discovered that God was already present in the place she feared would run dry. Her story reminds us that trust is a posture of the heart that releases what little we hold, believing God can sustain what remains. Before God multiplies resources, he often forms that trust, because only a trusting heart can carry provision without being consumed by it.

IV. GOD'S CONSISTENT STANDARD: *Justice, Mercy, and Care (Isaiah 58; Ezekiel 18; Matthew 25; Luke 3:11; James 2:15–16)*

Across Scripture, God defines righteous stewardship consistently as:

- Feed the hungry.
- Clothe the naked.
- Care for the widow and the orphan.
- Refuse to exploit or oppress others.
- Share what you have.

Jesus himself taught that nations would be judged by how they treated "the least of these."

Lesson #4

Wealth that ignores the suffering of others fails its divine purpose. True faith expresses itself through tangible mercy.

When God calls us to care for the poor, the vulnerable, and the forgotten, he is not simply issuing a moral command; he is forming our hearts. Generosity bends our instincts away from self-protection and toward love. Mercy loosens the grip of fear. When resources begin to move outward, they stop pretending to be our savior. In learning to see the "least of these," we learn to see as God sees, and our wealth becomes a servant of his purposes instead of a substitute for his presence.

V. THE WOMEN WHO FUNDED JESUS' MINISTRY: *Wealth as Support (Luke 8:1–3)*

As Jesus traveled from town to town preaching the kingdom, he did not do so alone. Luke records that alongside the twelve disciples were women—Mary Magdalene, Joanna, Susanna, and others—who supported him out of their own resources. They were not preaching publicly or standing in crowds. They were underwriting the mission itself. Their giving was not seen; but without their stewardship, the ministry would have stalled.

Lesson #5

God allows some to give of their wealth "unseen" so the Gospel can move freely.

These women remind us that calling is not always public, and stewardship is not always visible. Faithfulness does not require a platform; it requires availability. Their resources built the road beneath Jesus' ministry, making space for others to hear, be healed, and follow. In God's economy, unseen generosity is never unnoticed. It forms the heart toward humility, keeps the spotlight on Christ, and teaches us that provision is most powerful when it serves the mission rather than the self.

VI. THE RICH FOOL WHO HOARDED: *When Wealth Refuses to Flow (Luke 12:13–21)*

Jesus told a parable about a man whose barns overflowed. Instead of sharing, he decided to build bigger barns and store everything for himself. He congratulated his soul, certain he had secured the future.

But that night, his life was required of him. Jesus declared: "So it is with those who store up treasures for themselves but are not rich toward God."

Like snow that does not melt and turns into ice, blessing that never moves becomes a burden we cannot carry into eternity.

Lesson #6

Hoarded wealth creates the illusion of safety, but it cannot secure the soul.

The rich fool's problem was not planning or storing; it was believing that barns could do for him what only God can do. Hoarding turns provision into protection and shifts our trust from the Giver to the gift. When resources refuse to flow, they begin to own us. Jesus' parable served to remind us that the safest place for our treasures is in God's purposes, not our stockpiles. Formation teaches us to release what fear wants to clutch, so that our resources serve life rather than pretend to save it.

VII. Zacchaeus: *Wealth Redeemed Through Repentance (Luke 19:1–10)*

Zacchaeus was also rich, but very differently.

A chief tax collector, he had enriched himself through exploitation. When Jesus passed through Jericho, Zacchaeus climbed a tree just to see him. Jesus stopped, looked up, and called him by name.

That encounter changed everything.

Zacchaeus did not wait to be commanded. He stood and declared, "[H]alf of my possessions, Lord, I will give to the poor; and if I have defrauded anyone of anything, I will pay back four times as much."

Jesus responded, "Today salvation has come to this house" (Luke 19:9).

Lesson #7

Zacchaeus remained wealthy, but wealth no longer defined him. Wealth surrendered became evidence of salvation, not an obstacle to it.

Zacchaeus shows us that repentance is not merely apology; it is re-orientation. The very things that once bound him became the means through which God healed him. Where greed once narrowed his world, generosity opened it. Salvation did not arrive because Zacchaeus paid his way into God's favor; rather, his open hands revealed a heart set free. The same Jesus who exposed the rich young ruler's attachment is the Jesus who released Zacchaeus from his. When wealth is surrendered, it no longer competes for our identity; it becomes a tool in the hands of a redeemed life.

VIII. BARNABAS: *Generosity in the Early Church (Acts 4:36–37)*

In the early church, Barnabas sold a field he owned and laid the proceeds at the apostles' feet. His generosity strengthened the community and became a model of unity and care.

Lesson #8

Wealth was not condemned in the early church; it was appreciated. When surrendered, it became a structural support for God's work.

Barnabas reminds us that generosity is not always dramatic; sometimes it is modest faithfulness. He did not give to be noticed; he gave because his heart was already free. Where Achan hid and the rich fool hoarded, Barnabas opened his hands and trusted God with the outcome. His gift strengthened the entire community, showing that when wealth flows through surrendered people, it becomes part of God's provision for many. Formation precedes generosity—and then generosity continues formation, shaping us into people who delight to participate in God's mission.

IX. ANANIAS AND SAPPHIRA: *When Wealth Is Used to Perform Holiness (Acts 5)*

A man named Ananias, with the consent of his wife Sapphira, sold property and presented part of the proceeds, pretending it was the whole. Peter made the issue clear: the money was theirs to do with as they wished. The sin was not withholding; it was lying. They wanted the appearance of generosity without the surrender of truth.

Lesson #9

Wealth used to fabricate righteousness corrupts the soul. God desires integrity, not performance.

Of all the lessons on preparing the heart for abundance, this one may provoke the most discomfort, because Ananias and Sapphira wanted the reputation of generosity without the surrender that generosity requires.

Their story reminds us that God is not impressed by appearances. He is never fooled by spiritual performances, financial displays, or carefully curated humility. He looks beneath the gift to the heart that offers it. After the snow melted, they treated the river they were given as if it belonged to them, siphoning off what they wanted before offering the rest to God. God can free any heart tangled by wealth, but he begins that work only where truth is welcomed.

X. TIMOTHY: *The Greatest Inheritance (2 Timothy 1:5)*

The Apostle Paul praised Timothy not for material legacy, but for faith passed down—first through his grandmother Lois, then his mother Eunice. Faith outlasts every financial legacy.

Lesson #10

Financial wealth without faith is fragile. Faith passed through generations becomes a river no thief can steal, no market can crash, and no famine can dry up.

Paul's inheritance flowed through prayer, Scripture, discipleship, and love… the kind of riches that shape the heart long before material resources ever arrive. In avalanche language, Timothy reminds us that the most powerful rivers are not financial at all. They are currents of faith, character, and conviction that nourish every generation they reach. Where money may fade, faith remains, sustaining families, guiding decisions, and preparing hearts to steward whatever God entrusts.

Closing Reflection

Jesus' words were never meant to condemn wealth itself. They were meant to expose the subtle power wealth has to compete for the human heart. Across Scripture, the question is never, "Did this person have riches?" but "What hold did riches have on this person?"

Taken together, these stories reveal a consistent pattern. Wealth magnifies whatever it finds. In a heart ruled by fear, it becomes hoarding. In a heart ruled by pride, it becomes performance. In a heart ruled by greed, it becomes exploitation. But in a heart surrendered to God, it becomes provision, mercy, justice, hospitality, and the steady advancement of his kingdom.

The issue has never been abundance.

The issue has always been attachment.

God is not looking for empty hands nearly as much as he is looking for open ones. When the heart is free, resources no longer compete with Christ for our identity. They become rivers through which his life reaches others.

9

Not Every Avalanche Is Divine

If you have made it this far, congratulations! You have already completed some deep heart work. Spiritual formation is never simple, and preparing the soul for abundance often brings us face-to-face with past mistakes and with painful questions about who we truly are before God.

This next chapter will not be easier, but it will be important. We need to face a difficult truth with honesty and gentleness. Sudden wealth does not always come to those who walk closely with God. As we mentioned before, just because God authored gravity does not mean that every avalanche originates directly from God's hand.

And when it does come by his hand, it does not always look the way we imagined.

At this point, it becomes necessary to separate prosperity from automatic divine endorsement by restoring clarity, without cynicism or any diminishing of God's sovereignty. Over the years, many voices have linked wealth and righteousness so tightly that believers are left confused when reality does not match the promise. God is not the author of confusion (cf. 1

Corinthians 14:33), and Scripture calls us to discern carefully what we label as "blessing."

Because this truth can unsettle and even discourage us, it deserves careful reflection before we speak further about God's divine avalanche. My hope is to deepen faith and help us see blessing through God's eyes, rather than through cultural assumptions or spiritual shortcuts.

One of the most troubling questions for believers who walk closely with God is this: "Why do so many people who do not seek him, honor him, or live by his wisdom seem to experience sudden and overwhelming financial gain?"

We all know the stories:

- A dishonest executive exits with millions.
- A reckless investor stumbles into fortune.
- A celebrity rises overnight and self-destructs publicly.
- A corrupt heir inherits wealth they did nothing to steward.
- A company profits enormously while mistreating workers or damaging communities.
- A gambler hits a massive payout, and spirals into addiction.
- A politician gains power and wealth through manipulation and favoritism.
- A criminal empire flourishes for years before justice finally catches up.
- A lawsuit delivers a windfall that the recipient is emotionally unprepared to handle.

If wealth were proof of righteousness, Scripture would be very different. Yet the Bible is clear: prosperity alone is not a sign of God's approval. Psalm 73 captures this tension perfectly. The psalmist confesses his confusion and distress when he observes that "the wicked prosper" while remaining arrogant, violent, and unrepentant.

> *"...But as for me, my feet had almost stumbled... For I was envious of the arrogant; I saw the prosperity of the wicked. For they have no pain... they are not in trouble as others are... Such are the wicked; always at ease, they increase in riches."*
> Psalm 73:2–5, 12

The psalmist further admits he began to wonder whether faithfulness had been pointless: "All in vain I have kept my heart clean." But Scripture never promises that wealth is reserved for the wise. What it does promise is this: wealth magnifies the condition of the heart that receives it.

Jesus said,

> *"For where your treasure is, there your heart will be also."*
> Matthew 6:21

The psalmist's struggle is deeply human: If the wicked prosper, what does righteousness even matter? But the turning point comes when he enters God's presence and sees with clarity. Wealth, status, and momentum can look like blessing from the outside; yet Scripture reminds us that these things simply reveal what already lives within. Jesus' words echo that truth: wherever our treasure settles, our hearts inevitably follow. Sudden gain exposes and amplifies what is already there.

To take this seriously, we have to step back and ask how the world actually works and why certain patterns seem to gather momentum, avalanche-style. These realities help us unlearn the assumption that prosperity automatically signals God's endorsement.

REALITY 1: *Wealth follows behavior, not character.*

Sudden wealth often flows toward traits that are morally indifferent, or even morally dangerous, when not governed by wisdom. An avalanche has certain identifiable characteristics to the naked eye: speed, risk, force, visibility, momentum, and appetite. These traits in themselves are amoral until a person directs them toward good or ill.

These are the same attributes that are rewarded in modern financial systems.

They are rewarded in entertainment.

They are rewarded in speculation.

They are rewarded in environments where velocity matters more than virtue.

Wise, discerning people tend to move differently.

They count the cost (Luke 14:28).

They move slowly.

They avoid spectacle.

They resist shortcuts and they prefer sustainability to explosion.

As a result, they are *less likely* to experience sudden wealth, because wisdom itself resists volatility. God is not withholding; wisdom is simply slower than greed. After all, growth is patient and avalanches are violent.

Reality 2: *Permission is not the same as provision.*

Because God honors human freedom, he allows people, righteous or not, to build, risk, invest, scheme, and strive. And because creation itself operates according to patterns of sowing and reaping—where diligence often produces reward and negligence brings loss (Galatians 6:7–9)—results frequently follow behavior, whether or not the heart behind those actions is aligned with God.

God has ordered the world with consistency; it runs reliably even for the unrighteous. But unlike the deists of the 17th century, who pictured God as a clockmaker who winds the mechanism and walks away, God is no absentee maker. As we explained earlier with gravity, he sustains it at every moment; were he to withdraw, it would not merely slow but cease to exist. As the Catechism explains, "With creation, God does not abandon his creatures to themselves… [he] upholds and sustains them in being, enables them to act and brings them to their final end" (CCC 301). This is *creatio continua,* the continuing work of his providence: the order he established he also holds in being, free to intervene at any moment. And because he upholds that order rather than suspending it, the systems of this world continue to produce results, even when the lives operating within them are disordered. As Jesus teaches, God "makes his sun rise on the evil and on the good, and sends rain on the righteous and on the unrighteous" (Matthew 5:45).

But free will cuts both ways.

The same freedom that allows people to build quickly also exposes them to spiritual collapse when character lags behind capacity. Wealth gained without formation often magnifies fear, pride, isolation, or self-destruction. In that sense, sudden wealth is no breach of God's justice; it simply brings the inner life into view.

So, when we see people racing ahead financially like an explosive dry-slab release, it does not mean God has favored them more deeply. It means they have activated forces that work in this world while sometimes neglecting the slow, unseen work of becoming wise, rooted, and whole. Prosperity is *permitted*, not *consecrated*. God may allow wealth to arrive suddenly, but permission is not the same as provision.

REALITY 3: *Sudden wealth reveals; it does not transform.*

This is where Sudden Wealth Syndrome often takes hold. Drawing from their institute work with newly wealthy individuals, Goldbart and DiFuria describe how sudden financial change can unsettle identity, heighten anxiety, intensify comparison, and strain relationships. Their insights reveal the emotional turbulence that often accompanies rapid shifts in wealth.

But spiritual formation invites us to look one layer deeper. These reactions do not arise simply because money arrived quickly; they arise because sudden abundance places pressure on parts of the heart that were never formed to carry it.

What psychologists observe as disorientation, Scripture often describes as exposure.

Money does not create character. It accelerates it. It functions like a magnifying glass over the human spirit and enlarges whatever is already present.

Greed becomes excess.

Pride becomes entitlement.

Fear becomes hoarding.

Insecurity becomes control and domination.

Wounds turn into addictions.

Isolation hardens into arrogance.

When sudden wealth falls upon an unformed soul, it does not bless; it reveals. As the Catechism of the Catholic Church teaches, the soul "refers to the innermost aspect of man, that which is of greatest value in him, that by which he is most especially in God's image" (CCC 363). The pressure of abundance reaches into that deepest center, where identity, desire, and trust reside… and draws hidden loyalties into the light. What was concealed in ordinary seasons is revealed under the weight of sudden abundance. Priorities that once seemed spiritual are revealed as transactional. Relationships that looked stable are strained. Motives that were partly mixed become painfully clear.

This is why sudden wealth can feel like both elevation and unraveling at the same time. The external world applauds the increase, while the inner world is cracking under the weight of it. What was manageable when resources were limited becomes unmanageable when every option is suddenly on the table.

Money has power, but it does not have the power to heal, mature, or sanctify the human heart. It cannot make us more grateful, more humble, more faithful, or more loving. It simply gives the heart more room to act out what it already believes. What was once restrained becomes visible under abundance. It is true that money can purchase access to care—to doctors, medicine, and treatment—and in that sense, it can support physical healing. But it cannot heal the deeper center of the person. It cannot restore identity, reorder desire, or free the heart from fear, pride, or attachment. Those movements belong to grace, not currency.

REALITY 4: *The faithful are often spared sudden wealth.*

This truth is difficult but merciful. Many people who walk closely with God would be *harmed* by sudden financial increase. Not because money is evil, but because the human heart is fragile. Sudden abundance can tempt us away from dependence, distort our sense of identity, fracture relationships, or blur the line between God's provision and our performance. What arrives too quickly can outrun the soul that must carry it. The wisdom writer prays honestly:

> *"[G]ive me neither poverty nor riches;*
> *feed me with the food that I need...."*
> PROVERBS 30:8

He is asking for a life paced by God... not by appetite, impulse, or pressure. Spiritual formation teaches us that abundance follows a law of balance, and every blessing carries a threshold:

Too much snow buries the unprepared.

Too little snow starves the land.

God often protects his children from avalanches they cannot yet withstand, not to punish but to preserve. He withholds acceleration so that roots can deepen. He slows the increase so that humility has time to grow. He allows seasons of "just enough" so trust can become muscle rather than theory. God's economy emphasizes stewardship, not spectacle. He forms slowly what he intends to sustain.

Sometimes the most gracious answer to our prayers for abundance is delay—not denial but delay for the sake of capacity. God is preparing us to receive blessing without losing our souls in the process. In his timing, provision becomes partnership rather than pressure, and blessing becomes a river rather than a flood.

Reality 5: *Not every avalanche is from God.*

While some avalanches are acts of God, others are the result of unstable systems, unchecked momentum, and human pride.

God sometimes elevates suddenly: look at Joseph, Esther, or Daniel.

More often, he prepares cautiously: like David, Moses, or the disciples.

Sudden wealth without formation exposes more than it blesses. This is why it appears so frequently among the unwise—not because God favors them, but because what is unanchored cannot bear weight.

Reality 6: *What looks like a blessing in motion may, in fact, be instability gaining momentum.*

It may appear that the wicked prosper more quickly. But what we are often witnessing is not favor; it is fragility under acceleration. The unwise pursue speed, and speed creates the volatility that creates avalanches. Avalanches destroy those without anchors. To understand why, we have to look beneath the surface, because every sudden increase is also a test of capacity.

Any capacity stress test asks one core question: Can you remain intact when pressure increases suddenly? To pass that kind of test, you not only need resources, but also anchors, like a stable foundation, structural readiness, emotional regulation, accountability and counsel, and a strong dose of humility. Stress increases weight, but the proud and the wise respond differently to the increase in load.

The proud lack preparation, then *concentrate* the weight until it eventually snaps under the load.

The wise prepare, expecting to *distribute* the weight so it does not break them.

Consider what happens when capacity is tested without preparation:

- ❄ A load-bearing wall removed before the roof is supported does not create space; it brings the structure down. The problem was never the roof. The problem was removing the support before the structure was ready.
- ❄ A surgeon handed a scalpel without training does not heal; he endangers the patient. The instrument is not at fault. The formation is absent.
- ❄ A pilot placed in the cockpit before logging hours in the simulator does not fly safely; he crashes. Speed without preparation is not courage. It is exposure.
- ❄ A dam built without spillways does not preserve the water; it eventually falls under the pressure. The water is not the danger. The absence of channels is.

❄ A bridge designed for ten tons does not safely carry forty. The collapse is not caused by the vehicles. It reveals that the structure was asked to bear more than it had been prepared to carry.

No one looks at these situations and calls them gifts. Everyone recognizes them as dangers. The instrument, the resource, the opportunity… none of it is the problem. The problem is the absence of the capacity to carry it.

Sudden abundance follows the same law. What arrives before the capacity to hold it exposes the weak layers, but also the unexamined fears, the disordered attachments, and the unstable structures that were always there, waiting for pressure to make them visible.

The wise may never make headlines, but they endure long after the avalanche settles.

Closing Reflection

Not every avalanche is a blessing, and not every delay is denial. Wealth, like snow gathered on the mountain, accumulates slowly before it ever moves; and when it does, it reveals the strength or weakness of what lies below. Sometimes it gathers through the simple laws of cause and effect. Sometimes it arrives so quickly that it exposes the soul rather than transforming it. God is not unjust in allowing sudden abundance to fall where it will, nor is he unkind when he withholds it for a season. Often, restraint is mercy and preparation is protection, especially when sudden gain would outrun character.

The invitation of this chapter is to anchor yourself in wisdom, humility, and trust, rather than to measure yourself against the prosperity of others. Then, when increase comes, slowly or suddenly, it will find you formed, rooted, and able to bear its weight without breaking.

Reader's Prayer: Discernment Before Sudden Abundance

Lord, everything I have is from You, and everything I become depends upon Your grace.
Thank You for the hidden work You have done within me—
for the seasons of waiting, the quiet acts of obedience,
and the formation that often took place long before I could see its purpose.
As opportunities begin to unfold, keep my heart surrendered to You.
Do not let me mistake movement for Your leading,
urgency for Your calling, or open doors for Your direction.
Grant me the wisdom to recognize the channels You have prepared
and the courage to follow them faithfully.
Teach me to release what I cannot rightly possess
and to steward what You choose to entrust to me.
Help me to hold every gift, every relationship, every opportunity, and every resource with open hands,
remembering that I am a steward, not an owner.
When abundance comes, protect me from pride, self-reliance,
and the illusion that I have secured these blessings by my own strength.
Guard me from fear that clings too tightly and from haste that scatters what You intended to nourish.
Give me discernment to distinguish between what leads to life and what only appears to be success.
Keep me from confusing momentum with faithfulness
or activity with obedience.
May every decision I make be guided by Your Spirit

rather than by pressure, comparison, or the desire for approval.
As the snow You have formed begins to melt into living water,
teach me to guide it wisely.
Let nothing You have entrusted to me become runoff
through poor judgment, distraction, or misplaced priorities.
Direct every opportunity into the channels You have prepared
so that what begins on the mountain may become nourishment in the valley.
Grant me the humility to pause before acting,
the wisdom to judge rightly,
and the courage to move when You say, "Go,"
and to remain still when You say, "Wait."
If You choose to send sudden abundance,
let it never terminate with me.
May every blessing become a river of grace that refreshes others,
honors Your kingdom, and brings glory to Your name.
I surrender the outcome to You.
Lead me with wisdom,
establish my steps,
and let every opportunity become an act of faithful stewardship.
Amen.

10

King Solomon: When Blessing Becomes Runoff

So what happens when an avalanche reaches the runout zone and the meltwater has nowhere to flow? As the snow begins to melt, everything depends on whether the water finds an established channel. Guided by the contours of the mountain, meltwater seeps into the soil, fills streams, and eventually becomes a river that nourishes the valley below. But when the meltwater cannot find an established channel, it spreads across the surface as sheet runoff. Fast, uncontrolled runoff strips away topsoil, cuts gullies, erodes hillsides, carries away nutrients, and often contributes to downstream flooding. Instead of soaking into the ground, the water is scattered and lost.

The same is true of blessing. Provision alone does not guarantee nourishment. Once abundance begins to flow, it must be guided with wisdom. What is directed becomes life-giving. What is left without discernment is easily dissipated. Wealth is never merely a gift of resources; it is also a test of judgment, surrender, and faithful stewardship.

Blessing and destruction are not opposites in nature; they are often the result of how force meets structure. Sudden financial abundance carries the same dual potential. What can nourish a household may also crush it. What can create freedom may also generate instability.

In the early chapters of this book, we met Abraham, a man who stood at the summit of a promise he would never fully see and who held blessing with open hands because the Giver was always greater than the gift. His story showed us what formation looks like *before* the avalanche releases.

The Bible also gives us another figure, King Solomon, who reveals something different and necessary—what can happen *after* the avalanche has already fallen, when blessing arrives in abundance, opportunities multiply, and the heart that once surrendered begins, almost imperceptibly, to close around the gift instead of remaining open to the Giver.

Abraham and Solomon are not opposites. They are the same avalanche at different stages.

One received the promise and kept his hands open.

The other received the fulfillment and slowly tightened his grip around it.

The distance between them is not talent or calling or even wisdom. It is the sustained posture of surrender, the choice made again and again across a lifetime to love the Giver more than the gifts he sends.

Solomon truly stands as one of Scripture's most sobering examples of blessing that became runoff instead of a river. He began with humility, wisdom, and a heart oriented toward God. When the Lord appeared to him in a dream, Solomon did not ask for riches or a long life, but for wisdom to govern God's people. Pleased with this request, God granted him not only extraordinary wisdom, but also unparalleled wealth, honor, and long life if he obeyed God (1 Kings 3:5–14).

At first, this avalanche of blessing nourished Israel. Silver and gold became as common as stone in Jerusalem (2 Chronicles 1:15). Solomon's wealth built the magnificent Temple, expanded trade, and established Israel's reputation as a prosperous kingdom. Like rivers flowing from the mountain, his blessings brought life to the nation.

But Solomon's story also shows the danger of misdirected flow. As his wealth grew, so did his compromises. Long before Solomon became king, God had established covenant limits for every king of Israel. In the King's Law recorded in Deuteronomy 17:15–17, the Lord required that the king be an Israelite, then forbade him three things:

1) He must not acquire many horses for himself or make the people return to Egypt to obtain them.
2) He must not acquire many wives for himself, or else his heart will be led astray.
3) He must not accumulate large amounts of silver and gold for himself.

But what did King Solomon do?

He accumulated silver and gold beyond measure, built fleets of trading ships, imported horses and chariots from Egypt and Kue, and gathered immense treasures.

He also multiplied wives and foreign alliances, and his heart gradually turned away from the Lord (1 Kings 11:1–4). What began as a blessing became a stumbling block. The avalanche that once nourished the land now threatened to bury him under pride, idolatry, and compromise.

If King Solomon was so wise, why did he fall?

God gave him extraordinary discernment, yet wisdom does not replace free will. King Solomon knew what was right; *he simply stopped loving what was right.* Wisdom can teach, warn, and remind, but the heart determines whether we obey. Solomon did not fall overnight. He drifted, one compromise, one political marriage, one rationalized decision at a time, pulled by comfort, pride, and convenience.

Abundance introduces another test: "Will I stay surrendered when I no longer feel needy?" We often imagine that more money, position, or stability would eliminate spiritual struggle. Solomon's life teaches the opposite:

Abundance multiplies whatever the heart already loves.

God had placed limits on Israel's kings, safeguards against self-sufficiency and divided loyalty. Over time, King Solomon ignored every boundary.

The lesson is clear: sudden abundance can become wasted runoff as quickly as it becomes a river if surrender and discernment give way to self-reliance. Wealth is a test as much as it is a blessing. If Solomon, the wisest man of his age, could stumble under prosperity, then we too must remain watchful, formed, and surrendered.

These are the dangers we must prepare for, so that what God sends to bless us does not become a stumbling block:

I. OVERSPENDING: *The Trap of Excess*

Danger #1

Quick money can disappear faster than it came.

Sudden wealth often tempts us to spend beyond reason. The first purchases feel earned—a reward for arrival—and each one resets the baseline of what seems normal. A larger home, a finer car, a standard of comfort that gradually becomes the floor rather than the ceiling. When spending is fueled by excitement or comparison instead of stewardship, blessings evaporate quickly. What begins as celebration can quietly become expectation, making yesterday's luxury feel like today's necessity.

> *"Precious treasure remains in the house of the wise,*
> *but the fool devours it."*
> PROVERBS 21:20

> *"A few days later the younger son gathered all he had and traveled to a distant country, and there he squandered his property in dissolute living."*
> LUKE 15:13

> *"The lover of money will not be satisfied with money; nor the lover of wealth, with gain. This also is vanity."*
> ECCLESIASTES 5:10

Even Solomon normalized extravagance with his abundance. Scripture records the staggering scale of it: gold shields hammered for his palace, an ivory throne overlaid with gold, drinking vessels of pure gold, and silver so plentiful it was reckoned "as common in Jerusalem as stone." What once felt like blessing slowly became expectation, and expectation turned to entitlement. Excess did not arrive all at once; it grew gradually, purchase by purchase, decision by decision, until Solomon no longer noticed how far his heart had moved from simplicity and dependence on God.

Beneath this pattern often lies a deeper issue: covetousness. Scripture warns plainly,

> *"You shall not covet your neighbor's house; you shall not covet your neighbor's wife, or male or female slave, or ox, or donkey, or anything that belongs to your neighbor."*
> EXODUS 20:17

Comparison is corrosive because it destabilizes the heart. We see a neighbor's luxury car or a friend's extravagant celebration, and something begins to shift—admiration turns into comparison, comparison into insecurity, and insecurity into competition and the desire to match or surpass what we see. Left unchecked, this not-so-subtle shift redirects our decisions. What should be guided by wisdom becomes driven by imitation.

We must resist the urge to consume blessings in ways that are unsustainable. To covet is to lose sight of our identity; it anchors the heart in worldly status rather than in God's covenant.

II. DEPENDENTS AND OPPORTUNISTS: *The Weight of Others*

Danger #2

Others may try to latch on, draining your blessing.

When you prosper, others may come with outstretched hands. Some are genuine, people with real needs or sincere hearts who rejoice with you. But others may see your blessing as their opportunity. They may appeal to guilt, manipulate emotions, or expect ongoing support without growth or accountability. What begins as generosity can turn into obligation, resentment, or financial strain if wisdom is not present.

> *"Wealth brings many friends, but the poor are left friendless."*
> PROVERBS 19:4

> *"Many seek the favor of the generous,*
> *and everyone is a friend to a giver of gifts."*
> PROVERBS 19:6

> *"See, I am sending you out like sheep into the midst of wolves;*
> *so be wise as serpents and innocent as doves."*
> MATTHEW 10:16

> *"Jesus answered them, 'Very truly, I tell you, you are looking for me, not because you saw signs, but because you ate your fill of the loaves.'"*
> JOHN 6:26

Solomon experienced this pressure as his kingdom prospered. The Queen of Sheba arrived with a caravan of camels bearing gold, spices, and precious stones (1 Kings 10:1–2). Surrounding nations sought treaties, marriages, and financial agreements. They came drawn by access to Solomon's wealth and influence, not by love for the God of Israel. The political marriages proved the costliest. Scripture records that his many foreign wives—700 wives of royal birth and 300 concubines—turned away his heart after other gods (1 Kings 11:3–4). In time, these relationships shaped his heart more than he shaped theirs. What began as diplomacy slowly became dependency, and dependency turned to compromise. Abundance widened his circle, but it also widened the number of people who expected to benefit from him. Generosity must be guided by discernment. Sometimes the most faithful act is a firm, loving boundary rather than another gift—one that protects both the giver and the one asking.

III. INFLATED EGO: *Pride Before the Fall*

Danger #3

Wealth can tempt you into pride or a false sense of security.

Wealth can easily lead to pride, making us believe we achieved it by our own hand. But pride blinds us to God's grace.

> *"Do not say to yourself, 'My power and the might of my own hand have gotten me this wealth.' But remember the Lord your God, for it is he who gives you power to get wealth, so that he may confirm his covenant that he swore to your ancestors, as he is doing today."*
> DEUTERONOMY 8:17–18

> *"Pride goes before destruction, and a haughty spirit before a fall."*
> PROVERBS 16:18

> *"God opposes the proud, but gives grace to the humble."*
> JAMES 4:6

Solomon's life illustrates this danger vividly. As his success increased, so did his confidence in his own power and diplomacy. He spent seven years building the Temple, then spent thirteen years building his own palace—nearly twice the length of time and resources it took to build the Temple (1 Kings 6:38–7:1).

Such abundance can quietly feed the ego: Solomon "excelled all the kings of the earth in riches and in wisdom," and "the whole earth" sought after his wisdom with extravagant gifts (1 Kings 10:23–24). The king who once prayed for wisdom began to rely on strategy and alliances to secure his future. Pride rarely announces itself loudly; it shifts trust away from God and toward self. The more Solomon built, the less he remembered who had built his life in the first place. Humility—like the observance of God's laws—is the safeguard of wealth.

Pride whispers, "I did this."

Stewardship remembers, "God entrusted this."

IV. MISMANAGEMENT: *Losing Through Neglect or Exploitation*

Danger #4

Neglect erodes gains, while exploitation loses them.

Wealth can be mismanaged in two directions—through neglect that lets it erode, and through exploitation, extracting more than a foundation can bear.

Money without planning slips away like sand through fingers. Neglected wealth erodes through ordinary, unglamorous channels—taxes that go unaccounted for, investments made without counsel, fraud that exploits the inattentive, and expenses that quietly outpace income. None of these announce themselves; they work slowly, while our attention is elsewhere. But God stays attentive; he watches how we steward what we are given.

> *"Know well the condition of your flocks,*
> *and give attention to your herds."*
> PROVERBS 27:23

> *"Moreover, it is required of stewards that they be found trustworthy."*
> 1 CORINTHIANS 4:2

> *"If then you have not been faithful with the dishonest wealth, who will entrust to you the true riches?"*
> LUKE 16:11

Exploitation is another matter. Solomon, with all his resources, eventually lost control of what he had built because of it. His building projects and royal household were sustained by heavy taxation and forced labor. The strain did not surface fully until after his death: when the northern tribes begged his son Rehoboam to "lighten the hard service" his father had laid on them (1 Kings 12:4), Rehoboam refused, and ten tribes seceded, splitting the kingdom in two. A reign that began in wisdom ended in a fracture that never healed. Scripture frames that division as God's judgment for Solomon's idolatry (1 Kings 11:11–13), with the tax revolt as its human catalyst.

Solomon's story reminds us that wealth is not self-maintaining; it must be tended like a field, or it will grow wild. Nor is wealth ever a license to exploit others for our own gain. When wealth is properly managed, good fruit is not found in the money itself, but in the character and stewardship that the money makes possible.

V. ISOLATION: *Distance from Community*

Danger #5

Success can distance you from people who were once close.

Sudden wealth can create a gap between you and those who once walked beside you. Loneliness becomes a silent danger because having enough money, resources, or influence can tempt us to be self-sufficient. Not only do we begin to feel we no longer need other people, but we begin to wonder who loves us and who simply benefits from us. We also hesitate to share our struggles for fear of sounding ungrateful. Most of us have had that moment when we opened up about something genuinely heavy, only to see an eye-roll or hear, "Well… that's a first-world problem." The phrase stings. It implies that blessing cancels pain and that provision erases pressure. And so, we learn to keep our worries to ourselves, carrying them alone rather than risk appearing spoiled or unaware.

Over time, isolation does not announce itself; it settles like dust on a windowsill, almost unnoticed. Days pass, and without meaning to, the heart learns to protect itself. It becomes careful and closes doors out of wariness. What once felt like connection begins to feel risky, and the soul starts to live a little farther back from the world. By the time we recognize it, the guarding feels normal… and the loneliness has learned how to hide.

"The one who lives alone is self-indulgent, showing contempt for all who have sound judgment."
PROVERBS 18:1

"And let us consider how to provoke one another to love and good deeds, not neglecting to meet together, as is the habit of some, but encouraging one another, and all the more as you see the Day approaching."
HEBREWS 10:24–25

"Two are better than one, because they have a good reward for their toil. For if they fall, one will lift up the other…."
ECCLESIASTES 4:9–10

As Solomon's wealth increased, so did the distance between him and the people he led. Royal courts replaced friendships. Conversations that once felt honest became filtered through protocol and politeness. Advisors learned to tell him what he wanted to hear, not what he needed to hear. Flattery took the place of truth. Over time, the voices that could challenge him grew quieter, and the ones that affirmed his every decision grew louder. The voice of Ecclesiastes, traditionally attributed to Solomon, is saturated with the despair of having everything but still experiencing the same comfortless isolation as those beneath him:

> *"Again I saw all the oppressions that are practiced under the sun. Look, the tears of the oppressed—with no one to comfort them! On the side of their oppressors there was power—with no one to comfort them."*
> ECCLESIASTES 4:1

Isolation did not happen overnight. It arrived gradually, through comfort, privilege, and the quiet belief that success made him untouchable. With each layer of wealth, the people around him grew fewer. And as his world shrank, so did his dependence on God. What began as blessing slowly hardened into self-reliance, and self-reliance led him away from wise counsel and eventually, away from God's heart.

But wealth is healthiest when it draws people together, opening doors for relationship, generosity, and shared flourishing. Rather than elevating one above another, it creates space for mutual support and shared purpose. When stewarded well, wealth does not separate—it gathers, strengthens, and gives life to the communities it touches.

Who are the trusted voices I will invite to speak truth to me, even when abundance arrives?

VI. LIFESTYLE CREEP: *Bondage in Disguise*

Danger #6

Raising your spending to match new wealth instead of growing wisely.

Perhaps the most subtle danger is lifestyle creep: raising your expenses to match your new wealth until you feel trapped again. Lifestyle creep rarely feels like a decision. It feels like a series of reasonable upgrades. The reliable car is traded for a nicer one, and within a year its payment is simply part of life. A larger home brings more space, and the space asks to be filled, furnished, maintained, insured. A first-class seat, booked once for a long flight, quietly becomes the only tolerable way to travel. None of these feels like excess in the moment; each feels earned, even sensible. But the new comfort becomes the new minimum, and the minimum keeps climbing. What once felt like a luxury becomes a baseline you can no longer imagine living beneath.

> *"But those who want to be rich fall into temptation and are trapped by many senseless and harmful desires that plunge people into ruin and destruction."*
> 1 TIMOTHY 6:9

> *"Do not store up for yourselves treasures on earth, where moth and rust consume and where thieves break in and steal; but store up for yourselves treasures in heaven."*
> MATTHEW 6:19–20

> *"Keep your lives free from the love of money, and be content with what you have; for he has said, 'I will never leave you or forsake you.'"*
> HEBREWS 13:5

Solomon is one of the clearest examples in the Bible of lifestyle creep. It did not look reckless or impulsive at first. It looked *reasonable*, royal, strategic—even impressive. His court consumed vast daily provisions (1 Kings 4:22–23); his income swelled to six hundred sixty-six (666) talents of gold a year (1 Kings 10:14); he commissioned gold shields, an ivory throne overlaid with gold, and drinking vessels of pure gold until silver was reckoned worthless in his kingdom (1 Kings 10:16–21). (Some scholars notice that Solomon's annual income—666 talents of gold—echoes the number later given in Revelation. Scripture does not draw the connection explicitly, but the resonance is a sobering one: the very abundance that signaled blessing became bound up with the appetite that undid him.) Each new acquisition—more gold, more grandeur, more of everything a king could command—reset the baseline of what royal life required, and the standard could only rise from there. What had once been abundance became obligation, a scale of living so vast it had to be sustained by the heavy taxation and forced labor that would eventually fracture the kingdom.

That is what makes his story such a warning: the creep never announced itself. A bigger house or a finer chariot is not freedom if it only re-enslaves you to the pressure of maintaining it.

CLOSING REFLECTION

God's desire is not merely to bless his people, but to prepare them so that abundance becomes a river of life rather than wasted runoff. Prosperity carries weight.

- ❄ Overspending can dissipate blessing as quickly as it arrives.
- ❄ Opportunists can drain the strength entrusted to us.
- ❄ Pride can convince us we no longer need God.
- ❄ Mismanagement can erode what was entrusted.
- ❄ Isolation can separate us from the community that keeps us grounded.
- ❄ Lifestyle creep can return us to bondage disguised as success.

King Solomon stands as a sober reminder that even the wisest can drift when blessing outruns the formation of the soul. The issue was not the abundance itself, but the direction of the flow. What was given to nourish the kingdom slowly became misdirected by pride, compromise, and divided loyalty.

Abundance requires surrender, boundaries, humility, and a heart that returns again and again to God as the only true source.

11

Covenant Planting Method: Ignatian Discernment in a Culture of FOMO

Opportunity creates a peculiar pressure on the human heart. When doors begin to open, the question is no longer simply, "Is this good?" but "What if I miss it?"

In modern language, this anxiety is often called FOMO—the fear of missing out. FOMO is essentially a misreading of the terrain. It assumes opportunity is scarce, timing is slipping away, and speed is necessary. But the mountain teaches the opposite. When snow becomes meltwater, urgency does not create life; it creates dispersion. Water that is not guided will scatter in every direction, much of it lost as runoff rather than formed into channels that lead to the valley. This is why discernment must govern movement. Without it, urgency turns potential into loss, and what was meant to become a river disappears into the ground.

The modern phrase was coined in 2004 by Patrick J. McGinnis while writing for the Harvard Business School student newspaper. In an article titled *"Social Theory at HBS: McGinnis' Two FOs,"* he described a growing anxiety among students who felt pressured to attend every possible event, opportunity, or social gathering. He introduced two related ideas: FOMO, the fear of missing out on experiences others might be enjoying, and FOBO, the fear of a better option, which can lead to decision paralysis as a person hesitates to commit in case something superior appears.

What began as a lighthearted observation about student life soon gained wider attention, especially as social media amplified constant comparison with the lives and opportunities of others.

Psychologists later studied FOMO more formally, linking it to anxiety, social comparison, decision stress, and consumer behavior. One of the early empirical analyses came from psychologist Andrew K. Przybylski (and his colleagues) at the University of Essex in 2013, who examined how social media environments intensify the fear of missing out (Przybylski et al., 2013). While the concept is now widely used in popular culture, its roots lie in this observation: when people believe that every opportunity must be seized immediately, urgency replaces discernment and comparison replaces wisdom.

Long before modern culture named the anxiety of missing opportunities, Christian spirituality had already recognized the same interior struggle and developed a framework for addressing it. In the tradition of Ignatius of Loyola, discernment offers the opposite posture of FOMO:

Freedom from disordered urgency.

In *Spiritual Exercises* ([169]–[189]), Ignatius teaches that the spiritual life requires careful attention to the movements of the heart. When sufficient clarity has been gained through the experience of consolation and desolation, the soul is invited into a more faithful form of discernment. In his words, one should decide "according to the greater inclination of reason, and not according to any inclination of sense."

At its core, discernment is the practice of recognizing what draws us toward God and what pulls us away. Ignatius describes these interior movements as *consolation* and *desolation*. Consolation deepens faith, hope, and love, and brings a sense of interior freedom and clarity. Desolation, by contrast, produces unrest, confusion, discouragement, or a subtle movement away from trust. Over time, these patterns become recognizable. What consistently leads toward greater love and trust, and "where reason more inclines," is to be followed; what leads away is to be resisted. The goal is a heart free enough to choose what God is truly inviting.

Yet discernment is not always straightforward.

Some decisions are not between good and bad, but between two good and worthy possibilities.

A parent may wonder, "Do I attend my son's state competition, or meet the bishop visiting our parish?" A business owner may ask, "Do I fund my friend's startup, or support a struggling ministry?" Both paths may be morally good. Both may appear aligned with God.

It is exactly in these moments that a complementary lens becomes helpful.

What I call the **COVENANT PLANTING METHOD** builds upon Ignatian discernment by introducing a simple diagnostic test. First, Ignatian discernment calls out clearing the path:

- ❄ Imagine choosing each option until "the soul is not agitated by different spirits, and uses its natural powers freely and tranquilly."
- ❄ Pray: "God our Lord, may you be pleased to move my will."
- ❄ Then ask, "Put into my soul that which I ought to do."

As with the Examen, we begin by welcoming the Holy Spirit to move freely within us.

Then comes the Covenant Planting step: *we temporarily remove one option in prayer by laying it on the altar momentarily and observing what rises within the heart.* The heart's response often reveals whether we are responding to God's invitation or to another master.

Three responses are possible. The removal may bring—

1) *Relief* or quiet ease. The removal brings an unexpected sense of freedom or ease. You feel lighter. This often reveals that the option was driven more by pressure, fear, expectations, or simple FOMO than by authentic calling. Such an opportunity can usually be released with gratitude and without regret.

2) *Godly Sorrow*. What rises is that you are genuinely sad to let the choice go because the choice could suggest a grace meant to draw you closer to God. Here we must look closer, because not every sense of loss means the same thing. But if the removal suggests a sorrow that comes from God himself, not from a disordered attachment, then it could mean you are dropping the better of two choices.
3) *Attachment-Grief*, or restlessness. It is a worldly sorrow that grasps, compares, and/or fears for status, identity, or control. If you immediately worry about your reputation by removing this choice, it is showing that your heart is clinging to something besides God. The rich young ruler felt this second kind of loss, and his attachment-grief exposed an idol to surrender. The Apostle Paul talked about this worldly sorrow in 2 Corinthians 7:10, and while he was referring to what rises in the heart in response to sin and repentance—not vocational choices—the underlying principle of discernment still applies. The first kind of loss is the ache of a genuine calling temporarily laid on the altar; the second is the panic of an attachment threatened.

Covenant Planting does not replace discernment; it refines it. Where Ignatian discernment helps us notice where *peace grows*, Covenant Planting helps us notice where *attachment is exposed.* Together, they reveal the same truth: God's guidance is rarely found in urgency. It comes in the slow reordering of the heart. By removing an option, we take one additional step toward clarity.

When I began writing this book (and set aside a sacred space in my home office that resembled a monastic cell devoted to prayer and writing), many opportunities arose to attend events at my local parish. Each one felt important, and each seemed more urgent than the last. The FOMO was real. Yet in prayer I sensed that God had asked me to write this book, and that I was called to finish the work he had begun in me. Choosing to keep writing was not a rejection of the Church; it was obedience to the assignment God had given me. However, I struggled with the fear of missing out on each event, and with the worry that my fellow parishioners—with whom I was planting early relationship seeds—would soon forget I existed. When I examined each option individually, both seemed to bring consolation. One path would lead to a completed book and a sense of accomplishment; the other promised the gift of much-needed friendships.

Both appeared good.
Both appeared life-giving.

And yet Ignatius warned that the enemy can disguise himself as an angel of light. Even consolation must be tested, because what feels like the pull of friendship may be partly the fear of being forgotten.

But when I developed the technique of Covenant Planting—temporarily removing one option at a time and noticing the three movements of the heart—something unexpected emerged: the absence of one brought a quiet sense of relief, while the removal of the other revealed a deeper sense of loss, but the loss was not grasping, it was that "aw, shucks… God put this vision in my heart and I really wish I could stay home and finish the book." There was no panic, no comparison, no fear of missing out—only a quiet longing that remained turned toward God. That was the option I could not set down without godly sorrow, and it became the clearest indication of where the Holy Spirit was inviting me to remain. That quiet sorrow ultimately led me to finish this book.

Covenant Planting, or anti-FOMO planting, is not to be confused with JOMO, the "Joy of Missing Out," a social-media term popularized by technology writer Anil Dash in 2012. JOMO describes the relief and satisfaction of intentionally opting out of the pressure to participate in everything, particularly in digitally mediated environments shaped by constant comparison. The idea gained traction in conversations about digital overload, mindfulness, and personal well-being. At its core, JOMO is about stepping back. Covenant Planting, however, is not about stepping back from opportunity; it is about discerning it before planting. While the Parable of the Sower depicts four soils, each representing the receptivity of the hearer's heart to the word (the seed), the Parable of the Talents calls us to invest faithfully what the Master entrusts to us (Matthew 25:14–30). Seeds are meant to be sown, not stored indefinitely.

Avoiding all opportunities in the name of peace is not discernment; it is a loss of focus. Skipping the gym once in a while may bring temporary relief, but abandoning the discipline of movement altogether weakens the body. So, too, the spiritual life requires intentional planting. Covenant Planting restores balance. The unformed heart fears missing out, so it plants everywhere—or avoids planting altogether. The formed heart trusts the season established under covenant and plants where God has given peace. In the language of the divine avalanche, wise planting establishes channels so that when flow begins, it carries life to the valley rather than disappearing into runoff.

Johnny Beloved and Opportunity

Johnny Beloved has access.
He has (or lacks) identity.
He has (or lacks) preparation.
Now the invitations intensify, and so Johnny wonders: Is this the right time to move?

And this is where blessing and danger stand closest together. When the door of opportunity opens, Johnny must count on discernment before movement. Opportunity reveals whether Johnny is free to make that call.

UNFORMED JOHNNY

The first "real" opportunity arrives on a Thursday afternoon.

"Need you. Big move. Limited spots. You in?"

Johnny's heart speeds up before his discernment does. He has learned to associate speed with blessing and confidence with credibility. He feels that hot, familiar pressure that life is moving without him. He tells himself he is being bold, generous, diligent. But beneath those words is one driving force: FOMO (fear of missing out).

Within forty-eight hours, Johnny has said yes to five doors:

- A high-yield syndication with tight liquidity
- A "creative" tax strategy that sounds too smooth
- A public sponsorship that elevates his image
- A startup round out of loyalty
- A speculative play because the room sounds certain

None of it feels sinful. It feels impressive.

Johnny does not evaluate character; he evaluates outcomes. He assumes that because something is profitable, it must be providential, forgetting that wealth often follows certain traits that are morally indifferent (or even dangerous), and that God may permit the unrighteous to prosper without endorsing them. The doors are open, so he treats them like assignments.

But instability gains momentum quickly—more through unexamined acceleration than blatant rebellion.

Within weeks, the inner tightening begins.

Capital calls come due.

Surprise taxes arrive.

Someone wants "one more round."

Subtle expectations come from friends who now see his capacity. Each door he has opened is now asking something back.

The syndication's tight liquidity means money he cannot reach when the tax bill comes.

The startup wants a second round "to protect the first."

His spending has quietly risen to meet his new standing—an even better car, the right dinners, the upgrades that once felt earned and now simply feel required. Friends who once called to talk now call to ask. And the more he is included, the more important he feels—until he realizes he has multiplied commitments faster than he can oversee them.

It is the misdirected flow, lived from the inside.

Lifestyle creep has reset his baseline without his noticing.

Opportunists have attached themselves to his capacity.

Pride creeps in because inclusion feels like importance.

Isolation follows because he does not feel permitted to admit that blessing has become heavy.

Money is not transforming him; it is revealing him.

The same insecurity that once hid behind restraint now expresses itself through overcommitment and image management. What looks like a blessing in motion is, in reality, a sheet runoff.

Then a verse from Mass surfaces—something about a camel and a needle. It does not land as abstract theology. It lands as warning.

Johnny is not being punished; he is being exposed. And for the first time, he begins to consider a sobering possibility—not every avalanche is from God. Sometimes the most merciful thing God does is spare the faithful from sudden wealth that outruns formation.

FORMED JOHNNY

So, before he evaluates the opportunity, he evaluates himself. He asks three simple questions:

1) Is this aligned with my mission and current assignments?
2) Is this wise in this season of my life?

3) What would obedience look like here: yes, no, or not yet?

These questions clear the ground for the deeper test. Johnny has learned Covenant Planting from a spiritual advisor. In prayer he removes one option and watches his heart, then removes the next. When he imagines letting the opportunity pass, he notices something unexpected—peace remains. He welcomes the stillness in his heart.

Johnny has set a personal policy: "I do not invest, commit, or give large amounts under urgency."

Urgency is no longer proof of importance. It is a signal to slow down.

He returns to his anchors. He seeks counsel. But instead of analyzing the fallen snow, Johnny now focuses on something new: direction for the meltwater.

If this opportunity becomes part of his life, where will it lead?

What will it connect to?

Will it strengthen a channel of blessing?

Or scatter his attention and resources into something unproductive?

He understands now that opportunity is not about deciding whether something can grow, but whether it can be guided.

And then he does something unpredictably strong.

"I'm honored you asked. I'm not moving on this right now."

There is no guilt in his chest, no panic, no fear of missing out. Because identity is settled. His stewardship does not require scattering seed everywhere. It requires planting where God has given peace.

He recalls a lesson from Bible study about King Solomon that produced restraint: Solomon kept building because the kingdom became proof of who he was. Johnny, however, has learned that who he is must come before what he builds. Before money moves outward, Johnny moves inward—toward surrender, clarity, and humility.

When opportunity comes, he still invests and he still gives. But now he no longer asks only, "What can this produce?" He also asks, "Where will this flow? What will it become? Who will it reach?"

Because he understands something he did not know before: what is not directed will not remain.

So he begins to establish channels—intentional pathways for where his time, resources, and influence will go. And when flow begins, it no longer scatters in every direction. It moves with purpose.

It is not frantic.

Neither is it pressured.

It is directed, focused, and guided.

That is how blessing becomes a river instead of runoff: not by chasing every opportunity, but by guiding what has already been released.

STAGE V

Multiplication

The River & Valley Phases

What Will This Blessing Become After the Avalanche Passes?

BEFORE we move into Multiplication, we need to see the journey clearly, because everything that follows depends on understanding what has already happened.

The money was released. Johnny did not earn the avalanche. He received it.

Access was established. He was brought into a position he could not create on his own.

Identity was confirmed. He had to decide who he was in the presence of sudden abundance.

Preparation began. His heart and mind were formed (or left unformed) to carry what had been placed in his hands. His relationships and boundaries were tested.

Opportunity emerged. The inheritance revealed doors that required discernment, diligence, and obedience—and established the direction in which what was released would flow.

At every stage, the question was never, "Will provision come?" The provision had already arrived. The question was always, "What will this become in my hands?"

Now we arrive at the answer.

The avalanche has already fallen. The meltwater has been guided. Now it must become a nourishing river. What was released must now flow with consistency, direction, and purpose—carrying life into the valley below.

The posture is set. In the chapters that follow, Johnny learns to carry what was given rather than consume it—to live from overflow instead of urgency.

In nature, the most important work of an avalanche begins after the snow stops moving. What once fell with force does not remain frozen or dramatic.

It settles.

It melts.

It transforms.

And then it flows.

This is where multiplication truly begins.

In God's divine avalanche, multiplication does not mean more avalanches arriving one after another. It does not mean constant breakthroughs, repeated shocks of provision, or perpetual intensity. Multiplication means transformation and distribution—the quiet, sustained work of blessing becoming life.

What was once released as snow has now become a river. And that river nourishes valleys, fields, families, and generations. The avalanche may happen once, but the nourishment can last for decades. Multiplication is often misunderstood as expansion for its own sake: more money, more influence, more activity. But in God's economy, multiplication is not excess; it is fruitfulness. It is what blessing becomes after it stops being dramatic and after it has been rightly directed.

In this metaphor, the avalanche represents release: sudden provision, breakthrough, relief, inheritance activated. Opportunity established direction. Now Multiplication sustains what flows through stewardship, stability, generosity, influence, and legacy formed over time. It is the difference between a moment that changes your circumstances and a life that nourishes others because of that moment.

In Chapter 2, when we watched Israel cross into the Promised Land, we saw faith as obedience meeting the force that God supplies, and the willingness to act when God invites movement. This truth must be held carefully.

Sometimes obedience looks like stepping forward into motion.

Other times it looks like remaining steady when nothing appears to change. Multiplication requires both. This phase calls for restraint as much as resolve. Multiplication is not about forcing growth, accelerating outcomes, or proving success. A river does not strive to become something else; it simply continues to flow within the channels that have been established. In the same way, blessing multiplies when it is released from control and guided by wisdom.

When God entrusts increase, he is not asking, "How fast can you grow this?" He is asking, "Can this flow without destroying you or others?"

This is where legacy is shaped. The avalanche has already fallen. Now we discover what it will become.

12

The Posture of Overflow

To lend is to live from overflow. God's intention is provision that equips people for generosity and influence. In Chapter 2 on Access, we mentioned Deuteronomy 28:12 to describe a people positioned to lend rather than borrow. It portrays a people resourced by God in such a way that they are able to strengthen others rather than live in constant need.

In biblical terms, margin and stewardship investing build the capacity—having enough not only to sustain your own household, but to come alongside others without collapsing under the weight. Under Preparing Financially, we observed the following Scripture verse:

> *"And God is able to provide you with every blessing in abundance, so that by always having enough of everything, you may share abundantly in every good work."*
> 2 Corinthians 9:8

This is also the posture of the river. What enters its flow is received and carried rather than held tightly. It is not driven by urgency or scarcity, but by consistency and trust. Overflow, by its very nature, is provision entrusted for others. Living as lenders rather than borrowers reflects a shift in orientation. Survival spending reacts to scarcity and urgency. Stewardship investing prepares for fruitfulness and continuity. One consumes what arrives; the other positions resources to flow, multiply, and bless over time.

It helps to keep the two aspects of lending apart. The first is a position: living as a lender rather than a borrower, free of debt and able to help. The second is an act of generosity, the loan to someone in need that expects nothing back. One is where we stand; the other is what we do for others from where we stand.

The New Testament gives the latter its sharpest expression:

> *"[L]end, expecting nothing in return. Your reward will be great, and you will be children of the Most High…."*
>
> LUKE 6:35

Here Scripture draws a careful line between a gift and a loan. A gift transfers what is given and asks for nothing; ownership simply changes hands. A loan ordinarily expects return. Yet when the loan is made to someone in need, Jesus strips it of the very thing that makes lending profitable: the expectation of gain. Lending to the vulnerable, then, is not an investment dressed as kindness. It carries no interest, no leverage, and no hold over the borrower—so it comes to rest very near a gift, distinguished mainly by the dignity it preserves in the one who receives it.

This stage of the divine avalanche creates the freedom to move through life with stability, reducing the burdens of dependency, compounding interest, and financial pressure. It is the freedom to remain steady, to give without fear, and to allow what God has provided to move outward with purpose. It has been the aim of this book to help the reader develop exactly this: a vocabulary of overflow that names and sustains that freedom.

PRACTICAL APPLICATION: Directing Overflow

Once overflow begins, the focus shifts from receiving to guiding, ensuring that what is moving flows with purpose rather than dispersing without impact.

What is not defined will scatter.
What is defined can be sustained.

The following five Overflow Postures mirror the five movements of the Avalanche Examen from Chapter 6—not by accident, but by design (yes, even I got this amazing reveal as I was writing this book). The Examen was *interior work*: recognizing grace, noticing where God is at work, recognizing what competes for our trust, practicing surrender, and releasing outward in generosity. The Overflow Postures, however, are the *exterior expression* of that same movement. What the Examen formed within, overflow now carries outward.

One is the soul being shaped.

The other is the shaped soul in motion.

Formation always precedes flow. What was practiced in the stillness of the Examen now becomes the posture of a life that has learned to carry what God releases.

Many financial systems begin with formulas: save this much, invest that much, spend the rest. Such guidelines can be helpful starting points, but they are not universal laws. Seasons of life differ. Callings differ. Resources differ. Some are called to extraordinary generosity. Others, for a season, must focus on rebuilding stability after loss. The goal is not to reach a predetermined percentage but to become the kind of steward who can faithfully discern where each dollar should flow. Overflow is not measured by how closely you follow someone else's formula. It is measured by whether what God entrusts to you is directed with wisdom, cultivated with patience, and released with love.

The five Overflow Postures are therefore not percentages to calculate but dispositions to cultivate. They describe how a formed heart learns to direct whatever has been entrusted to it.

OVERFLOW POSTURE 1—INTENTION: *Begin by shifting your mindset from survival spending to intentional stewardship.*

Survival spending seeks immediate relief. It asks, "How do I get through this month?" Intentional stewardship asks a different question: "What is God asking me to do with what he has entrusted to me?" This shift does not require abundance; it requires purpose. It begins by pausing before every financial decision, weighing long-term faithfulness over short-term relief, and allowing wisdom, not anxiety, to guide your choices.

In this way, money moves from being a tool for survival to becoming a resource for multiplication.

This is the exterior expression of the Examen's first movement: *gratitude.* The Examen begins by naming what has already been given.

Stewardship investing begins the same way, by recognizing that what flows through our hands is not ours to clutch but ours to direct.

Gratitude sees provision as a gift.

Intention positions it as seed.

And seed rightly planted, becomes the river.

OVERFLOW POSTURE 2—MARGIN: *Prioritize building margin in your life.*

Creating margin is creating breathing room between what you have and what you owe, between obligation and capacity. Margin restores clarity, reduces panic, and returns the ability to choose rather than react.

Margin often looks like *less*, not more: fewer commitments crowding your calendar, fewer expenses pressing against your income, fewer emotional debts created by saying yes too quickly or too often. It creates space to pause before responding, room to pray before deciding, and time to act from wisdom rather than urgency. Financially, margin may mean living below your means, paying down obligations that steal peace, or maintaining reserves so that an unexpected expense does not become a crisis. Relationally, margin may mean healthier boundaries, clearer expectations, and the freedom to give without resentment or fear. Spiritually, margin creates holy space where God's voice is no longer drowned out by noise, pressure, or constant reaction.

This is the exterior expression of the Examen's second movement: *awareness.* The Examen asks you to look back over your day and notice where God has been at work. But you cannot notice what you have no space to see.

Margin is what makes awareness possible, not only in prayer, but in every dimension of life.

It is the breathing room in which God's voice becomes audible again.

OVERFLOW POSTURE 3—LIBERATION: *Alongside margin, work toward reducing dependency.*

As margin grows, begin to reduce reliance on what gradually limits freedom: debt, credit, and systems that extract through interest, urgency, or pressure. These forms of dependency often promise access, but over time they narrow choice and keep you in a reactive posture. Dependency keeps you responding to what is owed. Margin allows you to respond from what is available.

This shift is gradual. It may begin with paying down obligations, simplifying financial commitments, or resisting the pull of immediate access in favor of long-term stability. Each step restores a measure of freedom, space to act with clarity rather than compulsion. In this way, reducing dependency is not restriction; it is release. It allows what flows into your life to remain yours to steward.

This is the exterior expression of the Examen's third movement: *alignment*. The Examen invites the Spirit to reveal what competes with God for your trust—what you are afraid to lose or feel compelled to secure. Dependency answers that question in financial form. What we owe shapes what we fear. What we fear shapes what we choose. Liberation is not restriction; it is the exterior act of releasing what the Examen first named.

OVERFLOW POSTURE 4—CULTIVATION: *Position your resources to produce ongoing provision rather than one-time relief.*

The first posture was a shift in mindset. The fourth posture puts your resources to work. Here you direct your resources toward what endures. Rather than focusing only on immediate needs, begin to position what you have to generate steady, ongoing provision. This includes financial investments that grow over time, relational investments that deepen trust and strengthen community, and vocational investments that develop skill, excellence, and purpose.

Not every investment produces an immediate return, but wise investments create stability that compounds over time. And it is this stability that allows generosity to flow without strain or resentment. A life of overflow is not accidental—it is cultivated. When direction is set with intention, what has been released does not scatter, but continues to sustain.

This is the exterior expression of the Examen's fourth movement: *surrender*. The Examen does not ask you merely to let go; it asks you to entrust what you release toward its proper purpose. "Lord, where is this meant to flow? What is this for?" Cultivation answers that question financially. What is surrendered from fear becomes positioned for life. What was once held too tightly now compounds toward something that outlasts the moment of its release.

OVERFLOW POSTURE 5—RELEASE: *Allow what has been cultivated to flow beyond you.*

Intention reoriented the heart. Margin created the space. Liberation removed the obstacles. Cultivation produced what was needed. Now the fifth posture asks the final question: for whom?

Overflow that never reaches another person is not overflow; it is accumulation with better margins. A river does not exist for itself. It exists for what lies downstream—the fields, the households, the generations it nourishes long after the snow that formed it has been forgotten.

Generosity at this stage is not reactive giving, driven by guilt or pressure. It is ordered giving, the natural outward movement of a life that has been formed, freed, and made fruitful. It flows from discernment rather than compulsion, from abundance rather than anxiety, from calling rather than obligation.

The formed heart does not ask, "Can I afford to give?" It asks, "Where is this meant to flow?"

This is the exterior expression of the Examen's fifth movement: *generosity*. The Examen invited you to practice giving without recognition, to imagine a moment of abundance and choose to release it before you knew what would return. Overflow Posture 5 makes that imagination real. What the Examen rehearsed in prayer, a formed life now practices without thinking. Overflow creates excess that can be translated into almsgiving. Examples might include:

Meeting Someone's Immediate Needs

- Paying for someone's groceries at the checkout counter
- Covering a neighbor's electric bill
- Paying for someone's gas at the pump
- Covering the order for the car behind you at a drive-thru
- Paying for a single parent's laundry at a laundromat
- Purchasing school supplies for a child in need
- Buying a winter coat or shoes for someone who cannot afford them
- Quietly paying a family's prescription costs

Strengthening Families

- Helping a young couple with adoption expenses
- Providing meals for a family facing illness or grief
- Paying for childcare so exhausted parents can rest or attend counseling
- Assisting a widow with unexpected home repairs
- Helping an elderly neighbor with transportation or medical expenses

Investing in Someone's Future

- Helping a struggling student or supporting someone anonymously

- ❄ Paying a semester's tuition for a student pursuing their calling
- ❄ Funding vocational training or certification for someone seeking stable employment
- ❄ Purchasing tools or equipment that allow someone to start a trade or small business
- ❄ Providing seed capital for an entrepreneur of proven character

Supporting the Church and Mission

- ❄ Funding a missionary or ministry serving the poor
- ❄ Helping a church repair or expand its facilities
- ❄ Sponsoring a child's participation in a summer camp or retreat
- ❄ Providing Bibles for those who cannot afford them
- ❄ Supporting seminarians or religious vocations

Acts of Mercy

- ❄ Leaving an unusually generous tip for a server
- ❄ Paying off someone's layaway balance anonymously
- ❄ Sending an anonymous gift card to a family in financial hardship
- ❄ Replacing a broken appliance for someone living on a fixed income
- ❄ Covering funeral expenses for a family in crisis
- ❄ Mentoring someone without expecting anything in return
- ❄ Offering professional expertise free of charge to a nonprofit or family in need.
- ❄ Donating your time to tutor, coach, or teach practical skills.

Reader's Prayer:
Living from Overflow

Lord, order my life toward sufficiency and generosity.
Free me from fear-driven dependence and the anxiety of never having enough.
Teach me to steward wisely, so that what You provide may bless others without burden.
Form in me a heart that trusts Your timing, seeks Your wisdom, and refuses the shortcuts of worry or greed.
Where I have lived from reaction, give me rhythm.
Where I have lived from scarcity, give me margin.
Where I have lived from debt and pressure, give me freedom.
Let my resources reflect trust, foresight, and faith.
Make me a lender who lifts, not a borrower weighed down.
Let generosity become my reflex rather than my fear.
Direct what You place in my hands—
toward good work, toward people in need,
toward purposes that honor You.
Guard me from hoarding what was meant to flow,
and from giving in ways that harm rather than heal.
Shape my life to live from overflow, not lack—
That I may always be content, grateful, and ready to bless.
All that I have, and all that I am,
I place under Your direction and care.
Amen.

13

The Nourishing Rivers

When the snow finally reaches the valley, its journey is not over. The meltwater that has been gathered, tested, and guided now begins its most important work: bringing life.

A river does more than carry water. It nourishes fields, sustains communities, and creates conditions for future generations to flourish. The blessing that God entrusts to us is meant to do the same. It is not given merely for personal comfort or accumulation, but to become a source of life beyond ourselves.

Throughout this journey, we have seen that abundance requires formation before release, discernment after arrival, and surrender at every stage. The question is never simply, "How much has God placed in my hands?" but, "Where is he calling this blessing to flow?"

The avalanche's meltwater streams become the *nourishing rivers* of blessing.

In Psalm 46:4, the psalmist paints a similar picture: "There is a river whose streams make glad the city of God, the holy habitation of the Most High." Here, the river does not just flow—it revives and brings joy to the entire city where God dwells. As God reveals in the avalanche's cycle, blessing becomes most powerful when it moves beyond possession and becomes participation in his work.

But rivers do not form by accident. They flow where the ground has been prepared, where channels have been established, and where the weight of what was released can now move with purpose.

So, when God's blessings overflow in your life, they are not meant to stop with you; They are meant to reach others—strengthening households, creating opportunities, restoring hope, and nourishing the places God has entrusted to your care.

To make glad is to have the power to reshape households and awaken hope in others.

These rivers do not exist in isolation, nor do they arrive in perfect sequence. They often flow together, strengthening and shaping one another over time. What begins as provision becomes a system of life.

Let us examine these rivers of blessing:

I. DEBT FREEDOM: *Breaking the Chains of Bondage*

River #1

Freedom from financial constraints

One of the first rivers an avalanche can release is *freedom from debt.* In Preparation, we confronted debt as a threat to stability. Here, we see what happens when that burden is lifted. Debt is not only a financial burden, but also a spiritual and emotional weight. It steals joy, creates anxiety, and limits your ability to walk fully in the purpose God has called you to.

The Bible speaks plainly about debt:

> *"The rich rule over the poor,*
> *and the borrower is the slave of the lender."*
> PROVERBS 22:7

This verse makes it clear: debt places you under servitude. It limits your freedom and gives authority over your life to someone else.

> *"Owe no one anything, except to love one another; for the one who loves another has fulfilled the law."*
> ROMANS 13:8

The Apostle Paul reminds us that the only ongoing "debt" we should carry is the spiritual debt of love. Every other debt should be settled and cleared. God's design for his people is abundance, not enslavement. In his blessing, we are called to be channels of provision to strengthen and serve those around us. When God blesses you with sudden financial increase, you may finally see those chains of debt fall away. We all know well what a life in debt looks like because debt is built into the American economy. Banks, credit companies, car dealers, and even colleges profit from people owing them money. Borrowing is marketed as convenience, status, and opportunity, not risk.

And here is the real danger: over time, debt stops feeling like a warning sign and starts feeling like normal life. But a life propped up by borrowing is not freedom; it is a counterfeit version of it. And a counterfeit life cannot sustain peace.

Imagine living without the monthly weight of credit cards, student loans, car payments, or overdue bills. Picture opening your mailbox and not bracing yourself for another late notice, or logging into your bank account and seeing surplus instead of anxiety. Maybe that increase allows you to pay off the lingering medical bill that has followed you for years. Maybe it gives you the ability to catch up on a mortgage payment and finally breathe again.

For some, that blessing becomes the first emergency fund they have ever had, a cushion that means one broken appliance or unexpected car repair can no longer threaten stability. For others, it may mean setting aside college funds, saving toward retirement, or simply having the ability to say yes when God prompts generosity instead of worrying about how to cover next month's interest.

But debt freedom is more than financial relief; it is mental and spiritual liberation. Debt freedom does more than relieve pressure. It gives the person dominion over their finances and resources so that a job loss becomes a challenge rather than a catastrophe and a medical bill becomes manageable rather than devastating. Decisions are no longer driven by obligation, but by discernment. When the weight of debt is lifted, the soul regains the ability to respond thoughtfully rather than react immediately. You can care for your family, your aging parents, your children and grandchildren, and your home and obligations without worry or limitation.

Generosity is also easier when resources are available and under your control. When the enemy no longer uses debt as a whip to drive your decisions, you can stand taller. You can dream again. You can breathe again. Freedom from debt opens the door to new possibilities: peace of mind, the ability to give generously, and the courage to pursue God's vision for your life without being shackled to yesterday's obligations and constantly looking back in fear.

II. SECURITY: *A Safe Harbor for Your Family*

River #2

Resources for emergencies, healthcare, and stability for your family

The second river is *security*. With abundance, you can build an emergency fund so that a sudden illness, job loss, or unexpected expense does not shake your foundation. You can provide healthcare, education, and safety for your family. You can create an environment where your loved ones no longer live under constant stress.

This does not mean you will never face storms. Money is not a guarantee against problems, but it can provide stability. It means you will have the anchor and the resources to endure them without capsizing.

So, let us pause here for a moment. For many, this claim will feel counterintuitive. After all, it seems reasonable to assume that if financial pressure were removed—if there were enough money to solve problems, cover emergencies, and secure the future—peace would naturally follow. The fear of not being able to provide for one's family is real, and money does address real needs. It pays bills, creates options, and reduces immediate stress.

Yet what experience shows, and what Scripture not-so-quietly confirms, is that money often removes one layer of anxiety while revealing others beneath it. Financial abundance may quiet the fear of survival, but it can also introduce new fears: the fear of losing what you have gained, the fear of mismanaging it, the fear of betrayal, isolation, or the weight of decisions that now carry greater consequences. When the stakes rise, so does the weight of stewardship.

Peace of mind, then, does not automatically arrive with more resources. Unprepared blessing can feel overwhelming, even when it truly comes from God. His gifts are always good, but our readiness often determines how they feel when they arrive. True peace grows from formation, from ordered priorities, clear boundaries, and a heart anchored in something more stable than circumstances. Without that interior grounding, abundance can feel fragile, and provision can quickly turn into pressure instead of rest.

This is why security, as the second stepping-stone in spiritual formation, matters so deeply. Financial freedom can relieve many practical anxieties, but only when our inner life grows alongside it. Money can create stability, but only God gives security. Real peace rests not in what we possess, but in the one who provides.

True security is rooted in God's promises.

> *"And my God will fully satisfy every need of yours according to his riches in glory in Christ Jesus."*
> PHILIPPIANS 4:19

God is the ultimate provider. Financial blessing is not a replacement for him, but a channel through which his provision flows.

> *"The blessing of the Lord makes rich, and he adds no sorrow with it."*
> PROVERBS 10:22

> *"I will both lie down and sleep in peace; for you alone, O Lord, make me lie down in safety."*
> PSALM 4:8

Taken together, these passages remind us that true security is not found in money, but in God.

Wealth is a tool, but God is the fortress.

One supports… the other sustains. A fortress protects you when pressure comes. It does not move when circumstances change. A fortress also gives rest, identity, and safety.

Financial security may provide a safe harbor, but it is God's presence that ultimately anchors the soul as the source of stability, identity, and peace. "The Lord is my rock, my fortress, and my deliverer" (Psalm 18:2). Security, then, is not the absence of storms, but the presence of structure. It is what allows the river to continue flowing even when the weather changes.

III. FRUITFULNESS: *Seeds That Multiply*

River #3

Ability to invest in businesses, real estate, or education that multiplies wealth

Financial abundance also brings *fruitfulness.* Wealth is not only about what you spend; it is about what you plant. With resources, you can invest in businesses, real estate, education, or things that multiply wealth over time. Yet the fruitfulness Jesus describes begins much deeper than money. He illustrates it in the Parable of the Sower, told across three Gospels, each emphasizing a different dimension of fruitfulness.

Matthew highlights understanding and yield:

> *"But as for what was sown on good soil, this is the one who hears the word and understands it, who indeed bears fruit and yields, in one case a hundredfold, in another sixty, and in another thirty."*
> MATTHEW 13:23

Mark emphasizes perseverance under pressure:

> *"But they have no root, and endure only for a while; then, when trouble or persecution arises on account of the word, immediately they fall away."*
> Mark 4:17

Luke draws attention to the condition of the heart:

> *"But as for that in the good soil, these are the ones who, when they hear the word, hold it fast in an honest and good heart, and bear fruit with patient endurance."*
> Luke 8:15

The parable is not about the seed itself, but about the *preparedness of the soil.* God is the sower. The seed is his word. The soils represent the condition of the human heart. The harvest is the fruit that emerges through reception, perseverance, and formation. Prepared soil does not merely receive seed; it determines where growth is allowed to take root. In spiritual terms, this selective readiness is what we call fruitfulness: the God-given capacity, formed through preparation and discernment, to receive and steward what will bear life while refusing what will not. And the order matters: the capacity that the word forms in the heart governs every other kind of increase. A heart formed into good soil for the word becomes the only ground in which financial fruitfulness can grow without corrupting the one who holds it.

Earlier, we saw that opportunity discerns which doors to approach. Fruitfulness is what grows after the right doors have been chosen and entered. It allows you to say yes to what aligns with your calling and no to what distracts from it.

> *"In the morning sow your seed, and at evening do not let your hands be idle; for you do not know which will prosper, this or that, or whether both alike will be good."*
> ECCLESIASTES 11:6

Fruitfulness grows from discernment and diligence working together. Discernment comes first. It is the wisdom to recognize where to plant, which doors to approach, and which opportunities to refuse. Discernment prevents us from scattering seed everywhere out of anxiety or fear of missing out. It teaches us to listen, to test, and to wait for alignment rather than chasing every possibility that appears. The avalanche may have released the snow, but fruitfulness determines where that snow is allowed to take root once it settles.

Once discernment has chosen the field, diligence sustains the work. Diligence is steady faithfulness: showing up consistently, tending what has been entrusted, and refusing idleness even when results are delayed or unclear. How many of us abandon an endeavor simply because the outcome is not yet visible? Today, diligence often looks like grit—the kind of endurance my three sons learned through long marching band practices or early-morning swim laps, saying no to comfort in order to say yes to formation, without any guarantee of winning.

Discernment decides where to sow; diligence keeps us sowing without knowing the outcome. The sower is not asked to control the harvest, only to remain faithful in the work of planting while trusting God with what grows. That uncertainty is not a failure of wisdom; it is the very space where wisdom learns to trust God. Fruitfulness, then, is not forced or rushed. It emerges through disciplined effort guided by prayer, patience, and attentiveness to God's timing. Discernment directs the sowing; diligence tends the soil; and together they prepare the way for growth.

Fruitfulness, however, is never stagnant. In the life of faith, there is rarely a neutral holding pattern. What is alive is either growing or diminishing. When what we have been given is exercised, it strengthens. When it is ignored, avoided, or buried in fear, it does not remain unchanged; it slowly shrinks because unused gifts lose their vitality.

> *"For to all those who have, more will be given, and they will have an abundance; but from those who have nothing, even what they have will be taken away."*
> MATTHEW 25:29

This passage is a common stumbling point. Many readers hear these words and imagine a harsh God, one who rewards those who already have and strips even more from those who have little. But this parable is not a lesson in divine cruelty or economic favoritism. It is a lesson in stewardship, responsibility, and response to trust.

In the Parable of the Talents (Matthew 25:14–30), the master does not condemn the servant for receiving less. In fact, the servant with one talent was entrusted with an enormous sum, a fortune by any measure, as a single talent was roughly twenty years' wages. What separates the servants is not how much they were given, but what they did with what they received. Two servants engaged what was entrusted to them, taking faithful risk in service to their master. The third servant, driven by fear, buried the gift and refused responsibility altogether.

Jesus' statement that "to those who have, more will be given" does not mean that those who are wealthy will automatically become wealthier. It means that those who receive trust and respond with faithfulness are entrusted with greater responsibility. Likewise, "from those who have nothing" does not describe the poor, but those who refuse to use what they have been given. What is taken away is not livelihood, dignity, or worth; it is unused responsibility, withdrawn because it was never embraced.

In God's economy, multiplication follows stewardship. Growth requires engagement. Like muscles exercised at the gym, what is used strengthens; what is ignored or buried atrophies. God does not demand perfection or equal outcomes. He asks for participation. The tragedy of the parable is not loss, but the refusal to engage.

> *"So let us not grow weary in doing what is right, for we will reap at harvest time, if we do not give up."*
> GALATIANS 6:9

A river's power is revealed in what it sustains over time. What flows through it does not produce life instantly; it nourishes steadily, season by season. Fields are not revived in a moment, but through consistent watering, patient cultivation, and ongoing care.

Fruitfulness is not immediate; it is the result of sustained flow.

Seeds planted along the river's path require time, endurance, and faithful tending. Weariness often comes in the space between provision and visible harvest, when the work continues but the results are not yet seen. Yet Scripture assures us that persistence is never wasted. What is nourished in faith will bear fruit in due season—not according to our urgency, but according to God's timing. The harvest may be slow, but it is real. And it belongs to those who remain planted by the river and do not abandon the field before the season arrives.

IV. GENEROSITY: *Becoming a River to Others*

River #4

Capacity to give more to family, charities, ministries, or causes you deeply believe in

Perhaps the most beautiful river an avalanche creates is *generosity*. Suddenly, you can give not from scarcity, but from abundance. You can bless family members who are struggling, support charities and ministries, or sow into causes that matter to the kingdom.

Earlier we mentioned part of the Apostle Paul message, and here it is reminding us in full…

> *"You will be enriched in every way for your great generosity, which will produce thanksgiving to God through us; for the rendering of this ministry not only supplies the needs of the saints but also overflows with many thanksgivings to God."*
> 2 CORINTHIANS 9:11–12

God does not pour his blessings into your life so that you become a dam, holding back what was meant to move. Nor does he intend you to resemble the Dead Sea, where water flows in but never flows out, becoming so saturated with salt that no life can survive. Instead, God pours into you so that you might become a river, one that carries abundance beyond itself, flowing outward to refresh, restore, and give life to others.

One of my favorite illustrations comes from teaching tithing and generosity to children in Sunday school. I dipped a sponge into a bucket of water and lifted it out, heavy and dripping.

"What happens if you leave this sponge completely soaked in the sink and never wring it out?" I asked.

Even the sleepy students in the back sat up. A fifth-grade girl shot her hand into the air.

"I know!" she said. "It starts to stink!"

"Exactly," I replied. "Now imagine *we* are the sponge, and God is the one pouring resources into us. If we keep everything to ourselves—holding it in and never letting it flow out—we, too, begin to stink."

"Ewww," they replied in unison.

"But there is another problem with a sponge that stays full of old water," I explained. "There is no room left for anything new."

Silence.

"So, what do we have to do," I asked, "to make room for more water?"

"You have to wring it out!" one of the older kids cried out.

I squeezed the sponge, letting the water spill back into the bucket.

"Now," I asked, "is there room for fresh water?"

"Yes!"

"And that," I said, "is how money works in our lives. God pours into us, and we release what we've been given, through generosity and service, making room for fresh blessings before what we hold becomes stagnant, or like we said earlier, before we become stinky."

The greatest joy of abundance is the ability to give. Anyone who has watched young children bring their offerings to the basket on Sunday has seen this joy firsthand; they run, not walk, toward the altar, eager and unashamed in their generosity. Their delight is unmistakable.

Yet something often changes as we grow older. Adults tend to give more cautiously, sometimes with skepticism, hesitation, or even guarded resentment. When giving is shaped by a sense of scarcity, the heart begins to operate in fear, and anxiety naturally follows. True generosity, however, flows from trust, not calculation.

God encourages us to trust; not to hoard, but to flow like rivers into dry places.

> *"[G]ive, and it will be given to you. A good measure, pressed down, shaken together, running over, will be put into your lap; for the measure you give will be the measure you get back."*
> LUKE 6:38

Generosity is not a transactional promise to possess more wealth; we are not trying to leverage God or manipulate outcomes. Scripture never treats giving as a bargaining chip, but as a posture of trust. Generosity loosens our grip on fear and scarcity, reminding the soul that our security does not come from what we hold, but from the one who holds us. Generosity opens the heart to God's peace, aligns our priorities with his kingdom, and teaches us to rely on his provision, whatever form it takes. Sometimes God responds with material increase, sometimes with contentment, sometimes with wisdom or opportunities… but in every case, generosity reshapes the heart long before it reshapes the bank account.

> *"Each of you must give as you have made up your mind, not reluctantly or under compulsion, for God loves a cheerful giver."*
> 2 CORINTHIANS 9:7

> *"A generous person will be enriched, and one who gives water will get water."*
> PROVERBS 11:25

Generosity must also be guided by wisdom. Not every request is an assignment, and not every need is yours to carry. When something good is expressed in a distorted way, it becomes draining, reactive, chaotic, people-pleasing, and guilt-driven. Our inner thoughts convince us, "They need it, so I must give." True generosity flows from discernment, not pressure, ensuring that what is given strengthens rather than destabilizes.

In this way, generosity shapes the heart for abundance. It turns us from owners into stewards, and from reservoirs into rivers, able to let blessing flow rather than hoard it.

V. Creative Freedom: *Time to Build the Vision*

River #5

Time to write, create, or build the projects that matter most to you

Another river that financial blessing unlocks is *creative freedom.* When you are not crushed by financial survival, you have time and space to create. Whether you are a writer, artist, entrepreneur, or dreamer, money can buy time, the most precious resource of all. With this freedom, you can finally write the book, start the business, or launch the project God placed in your heart. Your mind is no longer consumed by bills; it is free to hear, imagine, and build. When financial stress lifts, your mind and spirit are free to create.

God's blessings often unlock gifts that were hidden under the weight of survival.

> *"[H]e has filled him with divine spirit, with skill, intelligence, and knowledge in every kind of craft, to devise artistic designs, to work in gold, silver, and bronze."*
> Exodus 35:31–32

In this passage, God fills Bezalel (from the tribe of Judah, son of Uri, grandson of Hur) with his Spirit for a purpose: skilled, disciplined craftsmanship for the building of the Tabernacle. The Spirit does not descend into chaos or idleness. He fills a person who is available, trained, attentive, and obedient.

This is the first time in Scripture that someone is explicitly described as being filled with the Spirit of God, and it is not a preacher, king, or prophet. It is a craftsman: an artisan whom God specifically chose to build the Tabernacle and its sacred furnishings.

Furthermore, God's Spirit empowers creativity when there is room for it—when the heart is ordered, the hands are practiced, and the work has been prepared. In Exodus, the Spirit fills Bezalel to animate what skill has already prepared. Preparation is the vessel through which inspiration arrives. Where there is order, humility, and readiness, the Spirit brings clarity, excellence, and life to the work. Divine creativity is the Spirit moving through what has been faithfully formed beneath the surface:

Just as snow must accumulate in layers, creativity requires structure.

Structure is what allows creative work to hold its shape over time. Without it, ideas dissipate the same way snow does without the right conditions to bind.

Just as channels must exist for meltwater to flow, inspiration requires formation. Inspiration without formation has nowhere to go. The channel is what gives the water direction. Formation is what gives inspiration its path; otherwise it scatters as runoff. And just as soil must be prepared before seed is sown, Spirit-led work requires capacity. The Spirit does not descend into disorder or idleness. He fills what has already been prepared—the trained hand, the ordered heart, the practiced skill. Capacity is the prepared soil.

> *"For we are what he has made us, created in Christ Jesus for good works, which God prepared beforehand to be our way of life."*
> EPHESIANS 2:10

The Apostle Paul makes clear that what "God prepared beforehand" does not refer to earning salvation through good works. Rather, good works flow from lives transformed by God's grace. The works themselves become an expression of that transformation, inviting us to participate in purposes God has already prepared, such as opportunities, responsibilities, and acts of service for his people. Creative freedom emerges within this framework. It is the capacity to align our gifts with God's assignment and to offer our work with focused attention and wholehearted devotion. Such freedom carries responsibility. It directs stewardship toward people, and enables opportunities and purposes that matter most.

VI. INFLUENCE: *A Seat at the Table*

River #6

A voice in decisions that shape communities

Finally, wealth can bring *influence.* Influence is the visible outcome of what has been formed in private. It reveals whether access, identity, preparation, and opportunity were stewarded well.

> *"Who knows? Perhaps you have come to royal dignity for just such a time as this."*
> ESTHER 4:14

Financial success often opens doors to places where decisions are made: boards, councils, partnerships, and community leadership. With influence comes responsibility—to be a voice of righteousness, to advocate for justice, and to shape culture instead of being shaped by it.

Influence is not about control; it is about stewardship. If God gives you a seat at the table, it is so you can represent his kingdom there. Influence must be stewarded carefully; it is not given for vanity but for purpose. Our question is never, "How can this benefit me?" but "How can this advance what God cares about?"

> *"You are the light of the world. A city built on a hill cannot be hid."*
> MATTHEW 5:14

Jesus' words remind us that influence is not something we choose once it has been given; it is something we steward. Light, by its very nature, reveals. A city on a hill does not announce itself; it is seen simply because it exists. In the same way, when God entrusts influence, provision, or opportunity to a person, visibility follows naturally.

Visibility, however, is not a reward. It is a responsibility. What is illuminated draws attention, shapes direction, and affects others, for good or for harm. Influence therefore requires intentionality, humility, and care. The higher the ground, the farther the light carries, and the greater the impact of every decision made there.

This is why preparation matters. Influence without formation can mislead, distort, or burn out. But when grounded in wisdom and anchored in God, visibility becomes a gift, not for self-exaltation, but for guidance and service to those who look toward the light for direction.

> *"When the righteous are in authority, the people rejoice; but when the wicked rule, the people groan."*
> PROVERBS 29:2

This proverb reminds us that influence is never private. Authority, leadership, and visibility always spill outward, shaping the lives of others, often in ways unseen by the one who holds power. When the righteous are entrusted with influence, the result is not applause for the leader, but *relief* for the people. Stability replaces fear. Justice replaces chaos. The community breathes easier.

Scripture does not describe righteous authority as self-advancing or self-protective. Its fruit is collective well-being. By contrast, when authority is used for self-glory, control, or personal gain, the weight of that misuse is felt by everyone beneath it. This is why leadership divorced from character produces groaning rather than rejoicing.

When God gives influence, therefore, it is not a mark of personal importance but a call to service. Influence is given so that others may flourish, not so the individual may be exalted. In God's economy, authority is measured not by how high one rises, but by how much life is made possible for those entrusted to one's care.

Every avalanche has rivers waiting below. What is released from the mountain does not remain at the summit, nor is it meant to pool in isolation. It flows outward into households, communities, and generations yet unseen.

What God entrusts to one life is always intended to bless many.

What began as a sudden release now becomes a sustained flow. The river does not exist for itself; it exists to nourish what lies beyond it. Fields are strengthened, homes are restored, and life takes root where the water continues to move. This is the ceaseless work of multiplication.

CLOSING REFLECTION

God's desire is not merely to release abundance, but to direct it so that what falls from the mountain flows outward into life. The six rivers of blessing require the same formation, surrender, and discernment that preceded the avalanche itself. But when they flow through a prepared and surrendered life, they become something extraordinary.

None of these rivers flows by accident. Each one is the fruit of what was formed in the snow phase, tested in the opportunity phase, and guided through the meltwater. Together they do not merely improve a single life; they reshape the landscape around it. But rivers that flow long enough do more than nourish the present. They carve the valley itself—embedding provision into the landscape in ways that outlast the season of release and the lifetime of the one who first received it. That is where we are headed next. We will see what the rivers leave behind when they reach the valley.

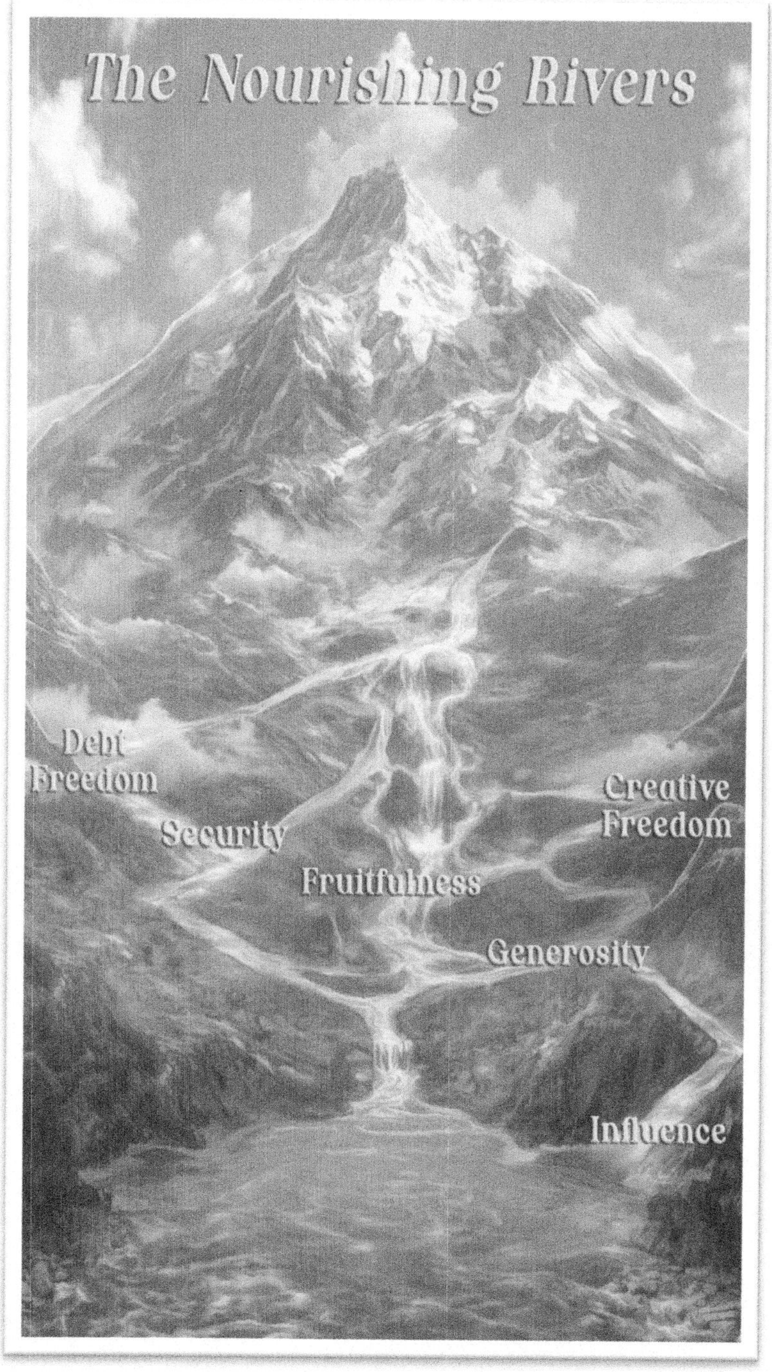
The Nourishing Rivers
Debt
Freedom
Security
Creative
Freedom
Fruitfulness
Generosity
Influence

14

The Legacy Story

God's blessings are rarely meant to stop with us. In Scripture, provision is designed to flow through one generation into the next, shaping faith, opportunity, and spiritual resilience long after we are gone.

We have reached the valley. What began as snow on the mountain has traveled the full length of the cycle—received, ordered, consecrated, rendered, reserved, and invested—and is now embedded in the lives of others. Provision that was once personal has become communal. Blessing that arrived in a moment is now nourishing what it was always meant to reach.

In Chapter 13 we watched blessing flow outward through six rivers—the active channels of a life living from overflow. Here we ask what those rivers leave behind when they have been flowing long enough to shape the valley itself. In the language of the river, what reaches the valley multiplies. What was once a single stream becomes a river of life for many. Families are strengthened, opportunities expand, and faith is carried forward through what has been faithfully stewarded.

Wealth rooted in wisdom and righteousness endures through generations, while wealth rooted in selfishness eventually erodes or passes into better hands.

> *"The good leave an inheritance to their children's children, but the sinner's wealth is laid up for the righteous."*
> PROVERBS 13:22

> *"…he commanded our ancestors to teach to their children; that the next generation might know them, the children yet unborn…."*
> PSALM 78:5–6

> *"Keep these words that I am commanding you today in your heart. Recite them to your children and talk about them when you are at home and when you are away, when you lie down and when you rise."*
> DEUTERONOMY 6:6–7

Over time, God has a way of redirecting resources toward those who will use them rightly—through consequences, social shifts, legal outcomes, inheritances, or the slow collapse of systems built on pride. This is not a promise of automatic transfer, but a pattern or a moral law woven into creation. Our task is not to control that movement, but to be ready for it; we must ensure that when resources come, they do not remain scattered on the mountain but are guided into the valleys below, where they can nourish, sustain, and multiply.

PREPARE GENERATIONALLY:
SHARE YOUR MISSION BEYOND YOUR LIFETIME

Stewardship does not end with provision; it extends into legacy. What God entrusts to us is not only for our present needs, but for future formation. What we do today will be forming a valley rich in heirs—ground where others can stand, grow, and flourish long after we are gone.

PRACTICAL APPLICATION: Preparing Generationally

If we desire our faith, values, and hard-won lessons to outlive us, we must begin preparing now—long before the next generation realizes how much they will one day need what we carry.

LEGACY MISSION 1—TESTIMONY: *Document your legacy story.*

Legacy is the intentional transfer of what matters most—faith, values, wisdom, lessons, and resources—from one generation to the next. Ask: "If my resources outlive me, what story do I want them to tell?" Write it down. Name the values, like faith, generosity, ministry, formation, education, service, and resilience, that you want to pass on to your heirs. You may borrow from mine:

MY LEGACY STORY

I want to tell you my story—not of accumulation, but of covenant. A story like Abraham, Isaac, and Jacob: of faith carried forward, of promises stewarded…

across generations,

across cultures,

across nations.

I want my life to be the story of a God who provides in ways we cannot foresee.

I want my heirs to tell the story of a Divine Avalanche—that God prepared me in a season when I was stretched to the breaking point: financially strained, navigating health concerns, walking through loss and grief, and searching for identity and access after so much had been shaken. It was a time when my husband stepped away from the security of tenure into the uncertainty of entrepreneurship, and when my sons were launching their own lives, needing more support than ever before.

And yet, it was there, under extreme pressure, that God was forming the ground beneath me.

When my resources outlive me, I want my sons to walk together in unity, establishing a family office guided not by impulse, but by counsel, prayer, and shared responsibility. I hope it will be sustained across time, with decisions shaped not by individual preference, but by collective discernment—investing wisely in family needs, extending generosity, pursuing creative projects and educational programs, and reinvesting in ministries and into communities with purpose. May the family office protect you against predatory lenders, and may the guardrails protect against false idols, impulse, exploitation, and want. May you be lenders and not borrowers, always expressing love beyond the tithe in merciful ways.

For my grandchildren and great-grandchildren, I desire something deeper than provision. I want them to be rich in formation:

to understand the value of an ordered life,

to love the Giver more than the gifts,

and to live within a rhythm of stewardship that meets their needs without distorting their hearts.

Above all, I want my life to bear witness to resilience, not as self-reliance, but as faithfulness.

That I endured,

that I wrestled,

that I stood firm through every trial, not because I was strong, but because God was faithful.

And when the story is told, let it be known: the avalanche came once and it almost destroyed us.

Greed almost overcame us.

We flipped houses instead of souls.

We allowed "lifestyle creep" to drown us.

We suffered from fear of missing out.

We anchored our identity in status and achievement, not in covenant.

But what did not destroy us made us stronger, taller, more resilient… to encounter the living Christ in the Blessed Sacrament.

So we prepared.

We reinforced.

And we conquered.

When the second avalanche came, it did not destroy us. It did not bury us, but settled us into the valley, bringing life where there was once fear. That is the proof I leave behind: a valley rich in micronutrients and abundance.

And let it be known… that evil did not overcome us—

that what God prepares today, he sustains beyond our lifetimes.

LEGACY MISSION 2—PROVISION: *Write (or update) your will.*

A will is an act of stewardship. It prevents confusion, protects loved ones, and directs resources toward God-honoring purposes rather than leaving decisions to courts. Writing a will and creating a legacy plan is not an exercise in control or pessimism; it is an act of love that extends beyond one's lifetime. Scripture consistently frames inheritance not merely as what is transferred, but as what is intentionally entrusted.

A will is the legal distribution of assets that gives shape to provision, protects relationships from confusion, and spares the next generation from bearing unnecessary burdens during moments of grief. A legacy plan or story leaves values, beliefs, teachings, charitable visions, family culture, and spiritual inheritance.

Generational planning also teaches something worth naming: that resources are meant to outlast us and stewardship is a mindset that can be passed on. When wealth is left without direction, it often becomes a source of division or waste. When it is ordered with clarity and prayer, it becomes a testimony—communicating values, priorities, and wisdom long after a voice has fallen silent. A legacy plan answers questions before they are asked and guides hands before they reach in uncertainty.

Beyond assets, what we choose to protect, how we distribute, and what we set aside reveals what we believe truly matters. A thoughtful plan creates continuity between generations, ensuring that provision supports education, health, opportunity, and generosity rather than self-indulgence or dependency. In this way, legacy becomes multiplication, not only of resources, but of stability, character, and purpose. Long-term readiness is an acknowledgment that abundance is never meant to end with us. It is meant to pass through us, shaped by wisdom, guided by faith, and released in a way that strengthens those who follow. To plan for legacy and asset management is to honor both the gifts received and the generations yet to come.

LEGACY MISSION 3—GUARDIANSHIP: *Establish beneficiaries on key accounts.*

Retirement accounts, insurance policies, and investment accounts often pass directly to designated beneficiaries, bypassing a will. For this reason, it is essential that these designations reflect your current intentions.

Beneficiary designations are not merely administrative details; they are acts of stewardship. They determine how resources move at a critical moment and can either preserve clarity or create confusion. Review them regularly, especially after major life changes, to ensure they remain aligned with your values, your relationships, and your broader legacy plan. This process can feel tedious—and at times frustrating—particularly when insurance companies are less than transparent about why you are calling or what information you are entitled to access. Persistence here is an act of stewardship. Push through the bureaucracy. What is at stake is too important to abandon at the first inconvenient phone call.

LEGACY MISSION 4—DISCIPLESHIP: *Build habits your children can imitate.*

Let your children see how you live, not just what you provide. Invite them into the rhythms of stewardship—budgeting, saving, giving first, forgiving when appropriate, and blessing others with patience and reverence.

What is modeled consistently is often absorbed unconsciously. Children learn not only from instruction, but from observation: what is prioritized, how decisions are made, and what is done when no one is watching. They notice the tone behind decisions, the posture of the heart, and the quiet disciplines that shape a life.

Legacy is not only transferred through documents; it is formed through daily habits. The way you handle money, extend generosity, and practice restraint becomes the pattern they carry forward. Over time, these small, repeated actions form a framework they will return to long after your words are forgotten. In this way, what you model today becomes what they normalize tomorrow.

LEGACY MISSION 5—CONTINUITY: *Start a family office, a foundation, a scholarship, or a trust.*

Sustained generosity rarely happens by accident. It is usually the result of structure. Foundations, scholarships, and trusts exist to give generosity a container, so that giving does not depend solely on emotion, memory, or the lifespan of one individual. Even modest resources, when set apart and governed wisely, can continue to bless long after the original giver is gone.

Many people imagine foundations as vast, institutional endeavors, but the principle behind them is available at any scale. Endurance comes from structure and clarity of purpose more than from size. A family might begin by funding a single scholarship at a local school, supporting one ministry annually, or setting aside a small trust to address medical needs, education, or faith formation. Over time, as assets grow or later generations participate, such efforts can expand. The largest and most enduring foundations show what structured giving can become. The Rockefeller, Carnegie, and Ford foundations were created by their founding families and trusted associates so that immense fortunes would serve a purpose beyond consumption and continue long after the ones who built them were gone. The same impulse works on the smallest scale: countless community foundations, church endowments, and scholarship funds began with a single family's decision to formalize their giving so it could outlive them. Many remain small by design, faithful and impactful all the same.

The goal is not to control your children's lives from beyond the grave. The goal is faithfulness past the reach of one's lifetime. A foundation or trust protects your generosity from running dry, spares your heirs from confusion, and gives future generations a shared mission to step into, one that invites stewardship instead of breeding entitlement. Generosity stops being a single act and becomes something closer to a practice: sustained and guided, growing over the years. To build a structure like this is to declare that what God has entrusted to us will keep serving others long after we are gone.

LEGACY MISSION 6—RIGHTEOUSNESS: *Use your influence to advocate for righteousness.*

What does that look like? Righteousness in Scripture is not abstract morality; it is right order in relationships with God, with people, and with institutions. To advocate for righteousness is to use whatever influence you have—social, financial, relational, or professional—to align systems and practices with truth, dignity, and justice.

> *"Speak out for those who cannot speak, for the rights of all the destitute."*
> PROVERBS 31:8

Influence, however, does not require a platform. It requires proximity and courage. Advocating for righteousness looks like the employee who speaks up when unethical practices are normalized at work. Or the swim mom and the soccer dad who refuse to participate in gossip or dishonesty. Or the person who asks hard questions at the HOA meeting about decisions that might harm the vulnerable residents of the community.

Righteousness often begins as quiet resistance, not loud protest. Sometimes it is just a matter of where your money, time, and attention flow. Like supporting organizations that protect families, educate children, or serve the poor; funding scholarships, apprenticeships, or recovery programs; or choosing vendors and partners who operate with integrity. This is righteousness expressed through allocation, modeling, intercession, and creating environments, and not through argument, sentiment, or cynicism. People learn righteousness less from instruction and more from observation.

LEGACY MISSION 7—FAITHFULNESS: *Show up consistently in places others abandon.*

Faithful presence itself becomes a stabilizing force and a powerful influence.

Good works falter not because of opposition, but because of abandonment. When attention fades, funding dries up, or progress feels slow… many withdraw, seeking places where impact feels quicker or recognition more visible. Yet Scripture and history both affirm that steadfast presence often accomplishes what urgency cannot.

To show up consistently is to lend weight to a place simply by remaining. It may look like continuing to attend a struggling church, school board meeting, or community organization when enthusiasm wanes. It may mean staying engaged with a neighborhood, ministry, or cause long after the initial momentum has passed. And you never know whether your consistent presence might be influencing others to raise their bars as well.

My husband's steady presence on the neighborhood HOA board no doubt has caused other residents to "lend their weight" more, to simply pay more attention, to show up more consistently, and to lean in more on discussions revolving around any new policy decisions or covenantal amendments that might affect them. That is because over time, this steady consistency builds trust, shapes culture, and steadies leadership. Leaders govern differently when they know someone is watching—not to criticize, but to remain.

Faithful presence also protects institutions from drift. When those who value truth and integrity stay involved, standards are upheld and excess is restrained. Influence grows not through control, but through reliability. People listen to those who have endured seasons of difficulty without leaving. In a world that rewards speed and novelty, consistency becomes countercultural. It signals commitment over convenience and responsibility over applause. Such presence rarely draws headlines, but it carries authority. And often, it is the very thing God uses to preserve what others would have given up on too soon.

LEGACY MISSION 8—READINESS: *Prepare for the appointed time.*

Do you recall meeting someone or facing a moment and thinking, as Mordecai reminded Esther, you may have come to your position *for such a time as this?* There are moments when preparation awakens responsibility, disclosing our purpose in this life. To recognize that God has been shaping you for a particular season is to receive an invitation into faithful stewardship. Such moments require humility, for the awareness of preparation can tempt us to magnify ourselves rather than the one who prepared us. Esther did not seek her position, nor did she fully understand its purpose when she received it. Only in the moment of crisis did its meaning become clear. Preparation often works this way: silently, patiently, and without explanation, until suddenly it is required.

If you feel that God has been preparing you for such a time as this, the question is not *why* you were chosen, but *how* you will respond. Esther's readiness was not proven by her access to power, but by her willingness to risk comfort for obedience: she fasted, sought counsel, and moved deliberately. Readiness, in God's economy, is marked by humility, courage, and restraint, not urgency or self-display, especially not the latter. This sense of calling is not about visibility, but alignment. The avalanche is the dramatic release, but the nourishing river is the subtle and understated purpose (and as we have examined, God positions people long before he reveals purpose). The task may be costly. It may require silence before speech. It may impose a long line or a crowded field. It may demand patience before action. It may ask for courage without guarantee. Yet Scripture reminds us that timing belongs to God, and readiness is his work, though we lean into it by participation and grace.

To be prepared for such a time as this is to stand steady when others panic, to act with discernment rather than impulse, and to trust that obedience—however tedious, insipid, or unseen—matters. When preparation meets purpose, God does not rush. He finds those who are ready… not because they chased the moment, but because they allowed him to shape them for it.

Johnny Beloved and Multiplication

The avalanche has already fallen. Johnny has the $7.4 million. The noise has quieted. The checks have been written (or withheld). Now the question remains: What will this become? Multiplication does not happen in the moment of release. It happens in what follows, when what is sudden becomes steady, when what is released begins to flow.

Twenty years from now, two very different valleys emerge. In one life, the inheritance is spent, diluted, litigated, or emotionally fractured. In the other, it is structured, compounding, teaching the next generation, and flowing beyond him.

The avalanche happened once.

In one life, it becomes erosion.

In the other, it becomes a river that sustains the valley.

Unformed Johnny

Johnny inherited $7.4 million. The noise of the moment quiets, the first checks are written, and the world moves on. But this is where the real test begins.

Multiplication does not happen in the moment of release. It happens in the months and years after—when what has been given must now be directed, sustained, and carried forward.

The question is no longer, "Did I receive?"

The question remains, "What will this become?"

And Johnny assumes the answer is simple: more. Unformed Johnny believes multiplication means expansion—more deals, more exposure, more access, more visibility. He upgrades quickly and calls it "growth." What he is really doing is converting a moment of provision into a permanent lifestyle without establishing the channels to sustain it.

He has a better house.

He has a higher monthly burn rate.

He displays public generosity at visible events.

He joins new social circles where bigger numbers are normal.

He loves the feeling of movement, but he never establishes direction. He does not create margin. He does not define channels. He allows what has been released to flow into the same patterns of impulse, image, and urgency.

So it moves, but it does not sustain.

At first, it still looks like success. Yet his posture quickly shifts from overflow to dependence. The money is no longer a resource to steward. Instead, it becomes a system he has to maintain.

He begins to give under pressure instead of calling.

He begins to invest from fear instead of wisdom.

He begins to spend from comparison instead of contentment.

And because he has not separated what is sacred from what is common, he cannot distinguish generosity from guilt, or fruitfulness from frenzy.

The rivers never form. What should flow becomes dispersion… runoff that never feels urgent but never stops either, because the slow hemorrhage never feels dramatic.

Instead of debt freedom, Johnny carries new forms of bondage—obligations, payments, and maintaining the life the avalanche has purchased.

Instead of stability, he carries greater anxiety, because the margin is thinner and the stakes are higher.

Instead of fruitfulness, he scatters seed everywhere, mistaking motion for harvest.

Even influence becomes weight, because visibility without formation does not feel like purpose; it feels like performance.

And something deeper is missing. Johnny never sees a need to pass on what matters most. He leaves instructions for assets, but not for the soul. There is no language of faith, no testimony of God's provision, no spiritual inheritance for those who will come after him. His heirs receive resources, but not direction.

Five years later, the result is not multiplication; it is maintenance.

Capital calls arrive at the worst times.

A venture fails.

A "helped" friend does not repay.

Family members begin to interpret love through money, and money through entitlement.

The inheritance does not unite; it strains and divides.

And twenty years later, the valley misses the opportunity to tell the story—not because Johnny is evil, but because he never guides what he receives. What is meant to nourish becomes erosion. What can sustain generations becomes diluted, spent, litigated, or emotionally fractured.

It is never about the amount. It is that Johnny tries to manage what he has never surrendered.

And he realizes too late what multiplication requires: you cannot multiply what you refuse to guide.

Without channels, the river becomes runoff.

Without margin, overflow becomes dependence.

Without stewardship, blessing does not become legacy; it unceremoniously becomes loss.

FORMED JOHNNY

Johnny inherited $7.4 million. The noise of the moment quiets, the first decisions are made, and life returns to normal. But Johnny understands something different now: multiplication is not growth… it is flow.

In nature, the most important work of an avalanche begins after the snow stops moving, when it settles, melts, transforms, and becomes rivers. In the same way, the question is no longer, "How much arrived?" but "What will this blessing become as it flows forward?"

The first year looks quiet, almost unimpressive to outsiders. Johnny does not rush to upgrade his life. Instead, he establishes direction. He understands that structure is not restriction; it is what allows blessing to move without destruction.

He pays off debt to break bondage rather than carry it forward under a new name.

He builds a twelve-month reserve so storms will not become crises.

He creates a "Divine Avalanche" account—set apart, not for display, but for discernment—so the blessing will not immediately enter circulation through impulse.

He meets regularly with his fiduciary and tax advisors, structuring his resources into clear channels, and making decisions slowly. He shifts from survival spending to stewardship investing. He prioritizes margin, because margin restores choice, quiets panic, and creates space for generosity without strain—so that giving flows from peace, not pressure.

Johnny tithes first. He gives intentionally. He invests patiently.

Urgency is no longer a spiritual signal; it is a warning light. He understands that the goal is not dependence but overflow: resources ordered in such a way that blessing can sustain good work without destabilizing the household. Instead of scattering seed everywhere, he plants where the soil is ready—discernment first, diligence second—trusting that fruitfulness is not forced; it emerges through steady stewardship.

His choices begin to shape rivers.

Debt freedom becomes real, not only as financial relief, but as mental and spiritual liberation.

Stability takes root, not as the illusion that money guarantees peace, but as a life anchored enough to endure storms without collapse.

Fruitfulness follows, because what is directed can now compound gradually over time.

Generosity becomes a channel rather than a reaction. He establishes a donor-advised fund so giving will remain joyful and guided, not pressured or performative. He creates a scholarship for first-generation college students—an intentional stream that will continue to flow long after the moment has passed. And as influence arrives (seats at tables, invitations turned into decisions), he treats visibility not as reward, but as responsibility, choosing righteousness and service over image.

What surprises most people is how little Johnny changes his lifestyle. Friends are confused. Some assume he is being overly cautious. But Johnny is at peace. He has learned that wealth without formation creates noise, but wealth guided by wisdom creates flow. He no longer needs money to prove identity, impress others, or relieve anxiety. He treats blessing as something sacred—something to steward, not to consume.

Five years later, the fruit is visible without being loud.

His capital has grown steadily.

His giving has increased quietly.

His scholarship has funded six students.

His parents' church has a repaired roof.

His investments produce income without pressure.

Johnny is no longer chasing avalanches. He is watching rivers. And what he establishes no longer depends on his presence. The rivers will continue even when he is gone.

But more importantly, something deeper is being passed on. Johnny does not leave only structured resources; he leaves understanding. He speaks openly about God's provision. He models restraint, generosity, and trust. He gives language to faith, so that those who come after him will not only receive blessing but know how to carry it.

The shift is internal as much as external. He no longer feels adrenaline around money; he feels stewardship. He does not feel powerful; he feels entrusted. Multiplication does not make him bigger. It makes him steadier.

The avalanche happened once. But in this life, it becomes irrigation, flowing beyond Johnny, nourishing others, and patiently shaping a valley that will sustain generations.

Epilogue: Standing at the Mountain's Base

Just as standing at the summit asks, "Who are you in God before anything moves?" the base of the mountain asks, "What will flow through you when everything does move?"

While this book has taken us all the way to the valley, most of us, in real time, find ourselves standing at the runout zone—the place where what has been released is first felt. The runout zone is the place of impact, testing, and stewardship under pressure. It is where the avalanche is no longer imagined but experienced, where blessing, crisis, or sudden change arrives, and decisions must be made with clarity and care.

Here, unprepared hearts can be overwhelmed, while prepared lives can begin to direct what has been released into channels of life. It is the ground where families, ministries, and futures are shaped—where the weight of what God allows becomes real. It is where theory becomes responsibility. Spiritually, this is where faith is revealed.

In the language of the avalanche, the summit is where God forms you; the runout zone is where he entrusts you. The valley, however, is where what you steward begins to nourish others.

And yet, I have come to believe that the real miracle is not the avalanche at all. What arrives suddenly can only be carried by what was built slowly. The true miracle is the quiet, patient work God does in the heart long before anything moves.

There were seasons when I prayed for increase, and God gave me discipline.

There were seasons when I asked for provision, and God gave me wisdom first.

And there were seasons when what I feared would bury me became the very thing that taught me to trust him.

In 2007, our family moved from Florida to Pasadena so I could attend Fuller Seminary. I longed to get my license as a marriage and family therapist because, like many, I had received well-meaning but inadequate church counseling. Fuller's integration of relationship psychology and faith felt like a gift from God—a way to help others with both professional skill and prayerful presence. I believed we were stepping into a new season of purpose.

What I did not see coming was 2008.

We owned several rental properties—investments we believed would fund college and retirement. When the market collapsed, our portfolio collapsed with it. I withdrew from my Marriage & Family Therapy program, completed a Master of Arts in Theology instead, and returned home to meet with realtors who slowly sold the properties one by one. The assets we thought were secure simply vanished.

We were not lazy.

We were not reckless.

But we were leveraged. The avalanche moved faster than our formation, and when that happens, even good things cannot hold.

Renting in California drained our reserves, and the losses felt relentless. It felt as though the ground beneath us had given way.

Looking back, the avalanche was not only financial; it was formative. What looked like collapse became instruction. We learned three things:

1) Leverage without margin is not faith; it is presumption. We assumed markets would always rise. God invited us to trust him instead.
2) Blessings turn destructive when they move faster than wisdom. We had opportunity, but not enough structure. God slowed us so he could steady us.
3) Loss can become mercy when it dismantles false security. What we thought we needed to feel safe, God gently removed… and we found him again.

After the properties were gone (and after a brief attempt at running a home staging company), I was in a car accident that aggravated undiagnosed spinal degeneration. The sciatica pain that followed lasted ten years. I grieved deeply. I gave up the dream of returning to California. I rewrote my will. I prayed from places of exhaustion, not theology. God received those prayers just the same. But his mercy found me, just not in the way I expected. A gifted orthopedic surgeon discovered that the issue was not my back, but my hips. After a double hip replacement, I could walk again. I could sit long enough to write again, this book included. Slowly, joy returned.

Somewhere along that journey, my husband and I began tithing again. We prayed the prayers you have prayed through these chapters. We practice the thirty-day pause rule on major purchases, allowing what arrives to settle. We sit with an Avalanche Examen to recognize what is gradually stirring in the heart before opening channels of blessing.

Essentially, we stopped chasing avalanches and started preparing our hearts.

We began to care less about what was *coming*, and more about who we were *becoming*.

Today, we are steadier, and steadiness has proven to be the greater form of provision. We know where our mountain truly is, and our children and grandchildren will inherit not just provision, but formation—roots that hold when seasons shift and winds rise.

We trust that God knows how to prepare those he intends to bless. Most of us may not have more wealth, but we will have more faith to stand with open hands, with a steady heart, with eyes that lock on the Giver and not the gift. For in the end, what defines us is not what passes through us but what is formed within our hearts.

Reader's Prayer of Readiness

Heavenly Father, I thank You that every blessing
comes from You, the Maker of heaven and earth.
You are my Source, my Provider, and my Sustainer.
I declare today that my heart is open, my spirit is ready,
and my life is surrendered to Your will.
If You send abundance, I will not hoard it;
I will steward it.
If You pour out wealth, I will not trust it; I will trust You.
If You give me influence, I will not boast in it;
I will use it to serve.
Lord, prepare me for the divine avalanche.
Anchor me in humility, surround me with wisdom,
and establish in me clear channels for what You release.
Give me discipline to manage what You entrust to me,
courage to give generously,
and vision to think generationally,
leaving rivers of life for my children,
my children's children, and those I will never meet.
Make me poor in spirit,
always aware that the Giver is greater than every gift.
May my avalanche never crush me,
but be guided into rivers that reach valleys beyond my sight,
watering lives, homes, and nations with Your goodness.
This is not for my glory, but for Yours alone.
In the mighty name of Jesus,
Amen.

Bibliography

Scripture

The New Oxford Annotated Bible with the Apocrypha. 5th ed. New Revised Standard Version. New York: Oxford University Press, 2018.

Theology and Spiritual Works

Aquinas, Thomas. *Summa Theologiae, Prima Pars, 1–49*. Translated by Fr. Laurence Shapcote, O.P. Vol. 21, Latin/English Edition of the Works of St. Thomas Aquinas. Green Bay, WI: Aquinas Institute, Inc., 2017.

Aquinas, Thomas. *Summa Theologiae, Prima Secundae, 71–114*. Translated by Fr. Laurence Shapcote, O.P. Vol. 16, Latin/English Edition of the Works of St. Thomas Aquinas. Green Bay, WI: Aquinas Institute, Inc., 2017.

Augustine of Hippo, Saint. *Confessions*. Translated by Edward Bouverie Pusey. London: J.M. Dent & Sons, 1907.

Augustine of Hippo, Saint. *On Christian Doctrine and Selected Introductory Works*. Edited by Timothy George. Nashville: B&H Academic, 2022.

Benedict of Nursia, Saint. *RB 1980: The Rule of St. Benedict in Latin and English with Notes*. Edited by Timothy Fry, O.S.B. Collegeville, MN: Liturgical Press, 1981.

Benedict XVI, Pope. *Deus Caritas Est*. Vatican City: Libreria Editrice Vaticana, 2005. https://www.vatican.va/content/benedict-xvi/en/encyclicals/documents/hf_ben-xvi_enc_20051225_deus-caritas-est.html

Cassian, John, Saint. *The Institutes.* Translated and annotated by Boniface Ramsey, O.P. Ancient Christian Writers 58. New York: Newman Press, 2000.

Catechism of the Catholic Church. 2nd ed. Vatican City: Libreria Editrice Vaticana; Washington, D.C.: United States Catholic Conference, 1997.

Cyprian of Carthage, Saint. "On the Unity of the Church" (Treatise I). Translated by Robert Ernest Wallis. In *Ante-Nicene Fathers,* Vol. 5. Edited by Alexander Roberts, James Donaldson, and A. Cleveland Coxe. Buffalo, NY: Christian Literature Publishing Co., 1886. Revised and edited for New Advent by Kevin Knight. https://www.newadvent.org/fathers/050701.htm

Evagrius Ponticus. *The Greek Ascetic Corpus.* Translated by Robert E. Sinkewicz. Oxford Early Christian Studies. Oxford: Oxford University Press, 2003.

Francis, Pope. "Blessed Are the Poor in Spirit." General Audience Catechesis on the Beatitudes. The Holy See, February 5, 2020. https://www.vatican.va/content/francesco/en/audiences/2020/documents/papa-francesco_20200205_udienza-generale.html

Francis de Sales, Saint. *Introduction to the Devout Life.* Translated by John K. Ryan. New York: Image Books/Doubleday, 1989.

Ignatius of Loyola, Saint. *The Spiritual Exercises of Saint Ignatius of Loyola.* Translated by Elder Mullan, S.J. New York: P.J. Kenedy & Sons, 1914.

John of the Cross, Saint. *The Ascent of Mount Carmel.* In *The Collected Works of St. John of the Cross.* Translated by Kieran Kavanaugh, O.C.D. and Otilio Rodriguez, O.C.D. Revised Edition. Washington, DC: ICS Publications, 1991.

John Paul II, Pope. *Redemptor Hominis.* Vatican City: Libreria Editrice Vaticana, 1979. https://www.vatican.va/content/john-paul-ii/en/encyclicals/documents/hf_jp-ii_enc_04031979_redemptor-hominis.html

Leo XIV, Pope. *Magnifica Humanitas: On Safeguarding the Human Person in the Time of Artificial Intelligence.* Encyclical letter. Vatican City: Libreria Editrice Vaticana, 2026. https://www.vatican.va/content/leo-xiv/en/encyclicals/documents/20260515-magnifica-humanitas.html

Pieper, Josef. *The Four Cardinal Virtues: Prudence, Justice, Fortitude, Temperance.* Translated by Richard and Clara Winston, Lawrence E. Lynch, and Daniel F. Coogan. Notre Dame, IN: University of Notre Dame Press, 1966.

Thérèse of Lisieux, Saint. *Story of a Soul: The Autobiography of Saint Thérèse of Lisieux.* Translated by John Clarke, O.C.D. 3rd ed. Washington, DC: ICS Publications, 1997.

Psychology and Behavioral Science

Bowlby, John. *Attachment and Loss,* Vol. 1: *Attachment.* London: Hogarth Press; New York: Basic Books, 1969.

Clear, James. *Atomic Habits: An Easy & Proven Way to Build Good Habits & Break Bad Ones.* New York: Avery, 2018.

Erikson, Erik H. *Identity: Youth and Crisis.* New York: W. W. Norton, 1968.

Goldbart, Stephen, and Joan DiFuria. *Affluence Intelligence: Earn More, Worry Less, and Live a Happy and Balanced Life.* New York: Da Capo Press, 2007.

Goldbart, Stephen, and Joan DiFuria. Money, Meaning & Choices Institute. Kentfield, CA. https://www.mmcinstitute.com

Lewin, Kurt. *Principles of Topological Psychology.* New York: McGraw-Hill, 1936.

Mullainathan, Sendhil, and Eldar Shafir. *Scarcity: Why Having Too Little Means So Much.* New York: Times Books, 2013.

Przybylski, Andrew K., Kou Murayama, Cody R. DeHaan, and Valerie Gladwell. "Motivational, Emotional, and Behavioral Correlates of Fear of Missing Out." *Computers in Human Behavior* 29, no. 4 (2013): 1841–1848.

CULTURAL AND CONCEPTUAL SOURCES

Dash, Anil. "JOMO!" *Anil Dash (blog)*, July 19, 2012. https://anildash.com/2012/07/19/jomo/

Fernandez Campos, Maria. "Self-Made vs. Inherited Billionaires: Global Ranking by Country." *DataPulse Research*, June 24, 2025. https://www.datapulse.de/en/billionaire-self-made/

McGinnis, Patrick J. "Social Theory at HBS: McGinnis' Two FOs." *The Harbus*, 2004.

"The Lottery Curse: Are Lottery Winners More Likely to Declare Bankruptcy?" *American Bankruptcy Institute (blog)*, Alexandria, VA. Accessed June 19, 2026. https://www.abi.org/feed-item/the-lottery-curse-are-lottery-winners-more-likely-to-declare-bankruptcy

Tremper, Bruce. *Staying Alive in Avalanche Terrain.* Seattle: The Mountaineers Books, 2008.

Vallery-Radot, René. *The Life of Pasteur.* Translated by R.L. Devonshire. 2 vols. New York: Doubleday, Page & Co., 1902.

About the Author

Frances Aurelia Newman was born in New York City to Cuban immigrants who fled Castro's regime in search of freedom and opportunity. She grew up in Miami, Florida, with a deep appreciation for resilience, faith, and responsibility—values that continue to shape both her life and her writing.

After studying journalism at Miami-Dade Community College, she spent a summer in Bologna, Italy, on full scholarship. She then obtained her bachelor's degree from New York University, where she cultivated a lifelong commitment to truth-seeking and clear communication. It was not until 2010, however, that she earned a Master of Arts in Theology from Fuller Theological Seminary in Pasadena, California. As part of a marriage and family therapy cohort at Fuller, she completed extensive coursework in family systems theory and family resilience—

integrating theological depth with a practical understanding of how families endure and heal.

Frances writes *God's Divine Avalanche* as the book she wishes she had read earlier in life. During seasons when God poured unexpected abundance into her household, particularly in the years leading up to the 2008 financial crisis, she and her husband found themselves entrusted with more than they were spiritually and practically prepared to steward. Then, when the financial collapse came, a lack of formation and readiness forced them to sell all of their real estate holdings, transforming what once felt like a blessing into a painful season of loss and recalibration. That experience became a defining teacher, shaping her conviction that sudden provision requires wisdom, preparation, and discernment if it is ever to remain life-giving.

After more than forty years as a devoted Protestant, Frances returned to the Roman Catholic Church, drawn by contemplative prayer, Eucharistic adoration, the spiritual writings of Henri Nouwen, and the sacrament of confession… where grace meets honesty and prepares the heart to receive the Eucharist. In these practices, she discovered a depth of spiritual formation she had long desired. Her work sits at the intersection of faith, formation, and financial stewardship, helping readers remain grounded when life changes faster than faith can easily interpret.

Frances lives in Florida with her husband and is the mother of three grown sons.

The author, age nine, at her First Holy Communion, St. Kevin Catholic Church, Miami, Florida, 1976, wearing a white alb, and posing with her brother, her parents, and the presiding priest. Miami was home to many first-generation Cuban Americans who passed the Catholic faith down through the generations.

For information about the *God's Divine Avalanche* Leader's Guide and resources for small groups or church-based study, please email:

divineavalancheinfo@gmail.com

REFRANCA
PRESS
2026
USA

Made in the USA
Monee, IL
04 November 2026

67383847R00203